AF412301

Development of Pragmatic and Discourse Skills in Chinese-Speaking Children

Benjamins Current Topics

Special issues of established journals tend to circulate within the orbit of the subscribers of those journals. For the Benjamins Current Topics series a number of special issues of various journals have been selected containing salient topics of research with the aim of finding new audiences for topically interesting material, bringing such material to a wider readership in book format.

For an overview of all books published in this series, please see
http://benjamins.com/catalog/bct

Volume 60

Development of Pragmatic and Discourse Skills in Chinese-Speaking Children
Edited by Zhu Hua and Lixian Jin

These materials were previously published in *Chinese Language and Discourse* 3:1 (2012)

Development of Pragmatic and Discourse Skills in Chinese-Speaking Children

Edited by

Zhu Hua
Birkbeck College, University of London, UK

Lixian Jin
De Montfort University, UK

John Benjamins Publishing Company
Amsterdam / Philadelphia

 The paper used in this publication meets the minimum requirements of the American National Standard for Information Sciences – Permanence of Paper for Printed Library Materials, ANSI z39.48-1984.

Library of Congress Cataloging-in-Publication Data

Development of Pragmatic and Discourse Skills in Chinese-Speaking Children / Edited by Zhu Hua and Lixian Jin.
p.   cm. (Benjamins Current Topics, ISSN 1874-0081 ; v. 60)
Includes bibliographical references and index.
1. English language--Study and teaching--Chinese speakers. 2. Second language acquisition. 3. Language acquisition. 4. Discourse analysis. I. Hua, Zhu, 1970- editor of compilation. II. Jin, Lixian, 1957- editor of compilation.
PE1130.C4D48   2014
428.2'4951--dc23   2014004753
ISBN 978 90 272 0279 6   (Hb ; alk. paper)
ISBN 978 90 272 7026 9   (Eb)

John Benjamins Publishing Co. · P.O. Box 36224 · 1020 ME Amsterdam · The Netherlands
John Benjamins North America · P.O. Box 27519 · Philadelphia PA 19118-0519 · USA

Table of contents

Development of pragmatic and discourse skills in Chinese-speaking children

Zhu Hua and Lixian Jin
Birkbeck College, University of London, UK / De Montfort University, UK

Defining aims

The development of pragmatic and discourse skills includes the learning of the communicative use of linguistic and non-linguistic expressions, interactional structures (such as conversations and narratives) and various contextually or culturally determined patterns of linguistic interaction to achieve communicative appropriateness and success. Recently, there has been a growing recognition of the centrality of pragmatic and discourse skills in children's language development (e.g. the special issue on conversation in language development and use edited by Veneziano 2010), due in part to their interface with other domains of language (such as syntactic and phonological domains) and to their clinical importance. It has also been recognised that children's pragmatic development starts surprisingly early, as soon as they begin to make active efforts to communicate their intentions by pointing and/or vocalising, which is ahead of their first recognisable words (Clark 2007). The lack or impairment of pragmatic and discourse skills has been regarded as a key clinical marker of several types of language and communication disorders (for a review, see Zhu Hua & Li Wei 2008). Pragmatic impairment also affects a small group of children who are otherwise normal on all the other clinical assessments (Bishop & Leonard 2000). However pervasive and important they are, pragmatic and discourse skills do not stand alone. They interact with various aspects of language capacity, including semantics, phonology, morphology, syntax, and, equally importantly, cognitive ability (the ability to understand intentionality and establish common ground, to map linguistic forms and functions, to understand and recall abstract concepts, etc.).

For many years, studies of the development of pragmatic and discourse skills in young children have predominantly focused on English and other European languages, reflecting the development of the field of child language studies in general. A limited number of published studies on Chinese-speaking children, however, have revealed interesting cultural and linguistic-specific patterns, demonstrating the needs for, and interest in, further research among these specific groups. For example, theoretically, research into the development of narrative structures by Chinese-speaking children shows some culture specific differences which may in principle reflect cultural practices in story-telling and can be seen in a broader context of metacognitive development and narrative learning (Cortazzi & Jin 2007). Hickmann & Hendriks (1999) found that Mandarin-speaking children are most likely to use null forms of references in narratives compared to English-, German- and French-speaking children when presented the same task of picture-description. Kyratzis & Guo (2001) found that contrary to the 'Separate Worlds Hypothesis' which posits that girls, through language, are more cooperative, Chinese girls share the same set of direct strategies in same-sex verbal conflict with U.S. boys, while Chinese boys use a combination of direct and indirect strategies. Zhou (2002) found that a task-oriented interactive model, rather than an adult or child-centred model, can offer a better description and explanation of the patterns observed amongst Chinese mother–child interactions.

This volume aims to further explore the development of pragmatic and discourse skills among Chinese-speaking children by addressing the following questions:

- How do Chinese-speaking children acquire pragmatic and discourse features which may be unique to the Chinese language(s)?
- How do socio-cultural and socioeconomic factors impact on Chinese-speaking children's development of pragmatic and discourse skills? Here, we will focus on maternal speech and seek to unpack features of the so-called *Chinese* style of parenting.
- How do children make sense of semiotic means other than linguistic ones? What narrative meanings can children make out of pictures, when presented with a picture story book?

Themes and Contexts in this volume

In this section, we will discuss each of the above questions in turn with the dual aim of providing a preview and context for each chapter selected for this volume.

Acquisition of language-specific features

Cross-linguistically, Chinese offers a unique opportunity to evaluate theoretical claims about language development which, up to the present, have been very often based on English-speaking children. Compared with English and other languages, Chinese has a number of oft-cited distinctive features. Apart from its writing system, these include its system of tones (distinct from Indo-European languages) and its limited range of grammatical and morphological markers (such as case, number and aspect markers), and its topic-prominent syntactic structure. In this collection, two chapters look into the acquisition of features specific to the Chinese language and culture. The first one, by Chiung-chih Huang, investigates the use of null forms and overt forms in self/other reference among Mandarin-speaking children. Unlike English which requires specification of the referent, Mandarin allows omission of reference to the speaker and the addressee in conversation, and speakers rely on situational and discourse contexts to disambiguate the implicit self-reference and other-reference. However, it has been observed that in the interaction between Mandarin-speaking children and adults, overt self/other reference forms coexist along with the null forms. Therefore, as Huang argues in her chapter, it will be interesting to investigate how overt and null forms are distributed within the child language in the Mandarin context and whether the distribution patterns match those of the mothers. Huang is also interested to find out whether Mandarin-speaking children's use of overt and null forms of self/other reference reflects their attempt to mark agentivity and control in a similar way as that shown in Budwig's work on English-speaking children (Budwig 1989).

Through a detailed analysis of recorded spontaneous interactional data between two girls with their mothers, Huang found a significant difference in the distributions of null forms and overt forms in children's speech: while overt forms occur more frequently in control acts (acts such as requests and warnings which aim to bring a change in the course of events), null forms appear more frequently in assertive acts (acts such as statements which describe an existing state). However, the same pattern is not echoed in the mothers' use of the self/other distinction. This suggests that the Mandarin-speaking children under study were able to make creative use of their own linguistic resources to mark the pragmatic functions of agentivity and social control. This lends strong support to the argument that children may have developed some understanding of the role of language in bringing changes to their environments and an ability to manipulate linguistic forms and functions to achieve their goals from an early age.

In the second chapter, Tse, Li and Leung investigate the use of expressions of time by 492 Cantonese-speaking children during free play sessions with their peers. While temporality is expressed primarily through the choice of tense of verbs in English, the notion is expressed through a combination of temporal adverbials, aspect markers, time expressions and contexts in the Chinese language(s). The complexity of forms and functions in Chinese temporality thus offers an opportunity to examine how children differentiate the nuanced discourse and pragmatic meanings carried by each form and how they match and coordinate multiple available forms to achieve the intended function. Generating a normative pattern of Chinese children's acquisition of temporality from a representative sample also has clinical implications. In English, difficulties with tense, aspect markers, verb agreement and auxiliary verbs have been regarded as some of the clinical markers for the presence of Specific Language Impairment (SLI). Several studies of Cantonese-speaking children with SLI (Stokes & Fletcher 2000; Stokes & Fletcher 2003) have reported interesting language-specific manifestations of impairment with regard to the use of aspect markers. The Cantonese-speaking children with SLI under study resemble normally developing children in frequency of use of aspect markers, but seem to limit their use of aspect markers to a small number of verbs. These exploratory clinical findings call for the need for baseline data, which now has been pioneered by collecting data from Chinese-speaking children in Malaysia for the development of a Chinese syntactic profile (Jin et al. 2012). Using a corpus-based approach and cross-sectional design, the authors of this second chapter establish a chronology of age of occurrence of a considerable range of temporal devices (consisting of 62 time expressions, 69 temporal adverbials and nine aspect markers) used by Cantonese-speaking children aged 3–5 in peer interactions, and they identify some common error patterns regarding temporality in the child language. These findings are interpreted in linguistic, cognitive and pragmatic terms.

Sociocultural and socioeconomic factors in development of pragmatic and discourse skills

Research evidence of the impact of sociocultural factors on children's language development, in particular, on pragmatic and discourse skills, comes largely from three separate yet interrelated fields. One is the linguistic research on cross-cultural variations of child-directed speech. A substantial amount of work in English-speaking contexts in the 1970s and 80s suggests that child-directed speech (also known as 'baby talk' or 'motherese') has many features that make them different from adult-to-adult speech. These features include exaggerated prosody, slower rate of speech, close alignment with the child's interests, and semantic contingency to the child's language through repetition, expansion and recasting (Ferguson 1964, 1977; Snow 1995). While these features suggest that adults fine-tune their speech according to their children's age and language abilities, how they adjust seems to be subject to cross-cultural variations, early work on which included children speaking such languages as Latvian, the Berber language of Morocco, and Kipsigis in rural Kenya (see studies in Ferguson & Snow 1977). On the issue of pitch variations, for example, a number of studies have identified patterns different from those among 'white middle-class American or European' parents. Ratner & Pye (1984) and Pye (1986) found that Quiche mothers in Guatemala rarely use high pitch when they speak to their babies. They in fact lower their pitch slightly when they speak to children, due to the fact that in the Quiche Mayan culture high pitch is very often used to persons of high status. Cross-cultural variations in pitch expansion are also reported by Fernald (1993), who found that Japanese and Mandarin-speaking mothers use a narrower range of pitch expansion compared with mothers speaking English and other European languages.

The link between child-directed talk and children's language development as well as the cultural impact on child–adult interaction have been highlighted in a second field, through the language socialisation research led by Elinor Ochs and Bambi Schieffelin (Schieffelin & Ochs 1986; Ochs 1988, Duranti, Ochs & Schieffelin 2012). Through compelling empirical evidence collected in anthropological traditions, the language socialisation work argues that:

–   Acquisition of sociocultural knowledge and acquisition of linguistic knowledge are interdependent.
–   Interactional routines and language use play an important role in socialising children into the society.
–   Language socialisation practices vary among communities, influenced by local cultural theories of child rearing which demonstrate wide-ranging differences in expectations and norms regarding when children should speak, how they should behave, and the nature of relevant cultural conceptions towards learning and child development.

In essence, language socialisation work envisages child-directed speech as an important channel of socialisation that plays an indispensible role in the child's process of becoming a competent speaker in the social world. In the last few decades, a growing amount of empirical evidence has accumulated on the culture-specific ways of language socialisation among less well-known and preindustrial communities such as the Samoan, Kaluli of Papua New Guinea, Kware'ae of the Solomon Islands, Basotho of Lesotho in southern Africa, etc. (studies of these communities can be found in Schieffelin & Ochs's edited volume in 1986 and a review can be found in Paugh 2012).

While child-directed speech and language socialisation research unpacked the role of child–adult interaction in child language development, an adjacent discipline in a third field, cross-cultural developmental psychology, has also turned to language to look for an answer. Taking a different trajectory from child-directed speech research, it starts with cross-cultural variations and similarities in developmental issues including cognition, personalities, emotions, behaviours and ways of communication, etc and seeks to address the question: To what extent, does culture impact on child development and growth (e.g. Bornstein, 1991)? In this field, which overlaps studies of the ethnography of childhood and parenting, language interaction is regarded as a key element in child care and interactive socialization (e.g. for detailed studies in Tonga in the south Pacific, see Morton 1996; and for research-based guidance for parents coming from the USA, Australia, Nigeria, the Ivory Coast, Indonesia, Turkey and the Western Caroline Islands in Micronesia, see DeLoache & Gottlieb 2000).

These three separate fields (child-directed speech, language socialisation, and cross-cultural developmental psychology) coalesce in the study of the issue of parenting style, in particular, how studies of maternal activities, responses and correspondences in mother–child interaction reveal different emphases of maternal speech and styles of maternal-child play. Following Bornstein's collection of cultural approaches to parenting, many cross-cultural comparative studies have been carried out to look for similarities and differences in parenting across cultures. For example, Shatz (1991) found that German mothers used more verbs with connotations of obligation and necessity than American mothers, and Vigil (2002) reported that while British mothers tend to respond to their infants' behaviours by following their lead, Chinese mothers directed their children's attention. Halberstadt & Lozada (2011) provide a review of cross-cultural variations in emotion development. In this collection, Zhuo Jing-Schmidt's chapter compares American and Mandarin Chinese mothers' 'affective' speech (i.e. speech showing mothers' approval/disapproval, admiration/disdain, appreciation/scolding, encouragement/criticism, etc.) in their interaction with children. Using data from existing corpuses in two cultural groups comparable in terms of play materials, gender composition and parental educational level, Jing-Schmidt compares the relative frequency of positive and negative affective speech acts in two groups. The results show that American mothers' speech is predominantly praise and appreciation of children's action and hard work, while Chinese mothers' speech is characterised by an emphasis on obedience and good behaviours and a predominance of verbal threats and scolding that are used to induce guilt and are seen as deterrence devices. These differences are interpreted in culture-specific ideologies and philosophies that impact on parenting style and ideas towards learning.

Group variations in parenting styles do not exist only between different cultural groups. Parental socioeconomic status (measured by income, educational level, occupation, etc.) within a given cultural community also matters. The need to look into socioeconomic factors in parenting styles is made pertinent partly by work carried out by Bernstein (1971), Bereiter and Engelmann (1966), and Labov (1972) which observed qualitative differences in language use between children from families with different socioeconomic status and resultant differentiation in academic success. Following this line of investigation, Zhou & Jing, in this volume, look into the relationship between Chinese mothers' educational backgrounds and their communicative acts in interacting with children. Using a considerable range of measures including the proportion of different types of social interchanges, frequency of different types of speech acts and pragmatic flexibility, and descriptive measures of utterances and turns, they found that mothers from a high education background and those from a low education background share a good level of similarities in terms of frequencies and types of social interchanges and speech acts. There are, however, significant differences in linguistic productivity, vocabulary diversity and pragmatic flexibility between the two groups. The maternal speech from those with a high education background is in general longer in mean utterance length and richer in vocabulary range and has greater pragmatic flexibility.

Understanding the process of meaning-making through pictures

Meanings are made and created not just through words, but also through different semiotic symbolic systems. Picture story books, where pictures interact with prints, have proved to be an important means of developing early childhood literacy. On one hand, eye tracking studies have found that young children spend a significantly longer time on pictures than on texts when reading story books (Justice & Lankford 2002). On the other hand, little is known about how children make sense of pictures in terms of narrative meaning. Many methodological challenges face researchers in this new, exciting area of research. For example, what analytical measures can be used to measure children's comprehension of pictures reliably?

The study by Li and her colleagues, reported in the last chapter of this volume, explores this issue. They adopt a story-retell experimental design to measure children's comprehension of pictures and develop an innovative analytical framework that integrates the key components of 'visual' grammar and 'story' grammar, two differing yet interacting semiotic systems embodied in a picture story book. The results show a clear age-differentiated pattern children's comprehension of pictures. Children as young as three years old demonstrate understanding of images of 'participants' such as characters, objects, etc. Their understanding of 'action event' (i.e. what story characters are doing) is comparatively weak in the youngest age group, but begins to improve around the age of four. The understanding of characters' states (i.e. what a story character looks like or how a character feels) is the slowest to develop across all the age groups. The slower pace of development of action events and, in particular, state of characters, as argued by the authors, is in proportion to the rate of development of inference and 'theory of mind' (i.e. the cognitive ability to infer mental states such as beliefs, desires, intentions, emotions, etc.) among children of the age groups under study. Li and her colleagues also offer some interpretations on why some pictures are more difficult to comprehend than others.

Looking back and looking forward

Having spent a good number of years researching on the Chinese languages and cultures, we found ourselves constantly pondering over one question. In global terms, there is an enormous number of Chinese-speaking children in China, Taiwan, Hong Kong, Singapore, Malaysia and among Chinese diasporic communities outside these areas, yet we know relatively little about how Chinese-speaking children acquire Chinese language(s) in normally developing conditions and when things go wrong (such as speech and language impairment, hearing impairment, autism, etc.) compared to English or other European languages with much smaller child populations. As we indicated earlier, studies of Chinese-speaking children are, however, important not just because this group is numerically significant world-wide but also for the linguistic typological and socio-cultural features associated with Chinese languages and cultures. Through our discussions with colleagues and publishers in various settings, it transpired that a number of factors might have contributed to this anomaly of the relative lack of research in this past. These include the lack of funding and resources; an under-developed culture of research in these fields in universities ('academic' staff in many universities in China lack dedicated research time in their work load and find themselves deluged with teaching and administrative commitment); a difficulty in accessing publications published in English due to the language barrier and lack of resources; and a lack of critical mass and networks with researchers who are scattered in a handful of universities and across a range of disciplines including psychology, linguistics, foreign language studies, preschool education, and special education; and challenges in disseminating research findings at international conferences and through publications in English-medium journals.

Having said this, we realised that things have recently been changing towards a positive direction. In the last couple of years, we have seen the launch of new academic journals dedicated to the Chinese languages and cultures, such as the journal *Chinese Language and Discourse* published by John Benjamins. There has been a wave of volumes dedicated to the language development of Chinese children published either in Chinese or English (e.g. Zhou et al 2010; Zhou 2009; Zhu 2002; Yip & Matthews 2007; Qi, 2011, Li Wei 2010; Jin et al. 2012). We hope that interest in the language acquisition of Chinese continues to expand with the growing demand for a better understanding of facts and factors in Chinese-speaking children's process of language development among parents, teachers, clinicians and policy makers.

This volume spins off a colloquium convened in AILA, Beijing, August, 2011, by ourselves and Zhou Jing from East China Normal University. The contributors of this volume are based in Mainland China, Taiwan, USA, Hong Kong and the UK. As editors, we are grateful to their effort and commitment. We are also grateful to the editors of *Chinese Language and Discourse*, Hongyin Tao, K-K Luke and Li Wei for their support since the conception of the idea for the special issue on which the volume is based on. We hope that it will be a significant addition to the research literature and help to draw attention to some pressing issues in the study of the acquisition of pragmatic and discourse skills, which is a promising field of interdisciplinary investigation.

References

Bereiter, Carl & Engelman, Siegfried. 1966. *Disadvantaged Children in the Preschool*. Englewood Cliffs, NJ: Prentice-Hall.

Bernstein, Basil. 1971. *Class, Codes and Control: Theoretical Studies Towards a Sociology of Language, Vol 1*. London: Routledge.

Bishop, Dorothy, V. M. & Leonard, Laurence B. ed. 2000. *Speech and Language Impairments in Children: Causes, Characteristics, Intervention and Outcome*. Hove, UK: Psychology Press.

Bornstein, Marc H. 1991. *Cultural Approaches to Parenting*. Hillsdale, NJ: Lawrence Erlbaum Associates.

Budwig, Nancy. 1989. "The Linguistic Marking of Agentivity and Control in Child Language". *Journal of Child Language* 16.263–284.

Clark, Eve. 2007. "Pragmatics and Language Acquisition". *The Handbook of Pragmatics*, ed. by Laurence R. Horn & Gregory Ward, 562–577. Malden, MA: Blackwell.

Cortazzi, Martin & Jin, Lixian. 2007. "Narrative Learning, EAL and Metacognitive Development". *Early Child Development and Care* 177:6–7.645–660.

DeLoache, Judy & Gottlieb, Alma. 2000. *A World of Babies: Imagined Childcare Guides for Seven Societies*. Cambridge: Cambridge University Press.

Duranti, Alessandro, Elinor Ochs & B. Schieffelin, Bambi. 2012. *The Handbook of Language Socialisation*. Malden, MA: Wiley-Blackwell.

Ferguson, Charles. 1964. "Baby talk in six languages". *American Anthropologist* 66 (6 Part 2), 103–114.

Ferguson, Charles. 1977. "Baby Talk as a Simplified Register". *Talking to Children: Language Input and Acquisition* ed. by Catherine Snow & Charles A. Ferguson, 209–235. Cambridge: Cambridge University Press.

Ferguson, Charles A. & E. Snow, Catherine 1977 *Talking to Children, Language Input and Acquisition*. Cambridge: Cambridge University Press.

Fernald, Anne. 1993. "Human Maternal Vocalizations to Infants as Biologically Relevant Signals: An Evolutionary Perspective". *Language Acquisition: Core Readings* ed. by Paul Bloom, 51–94. New York: Harvester Wheatsheaf.

Halberstadt, Amy G. & Y. Lozada, Fantasy. 2011. "Emotion Development in Infancy through the Lens of Culture". *Emotion Review* 3.158–168.

Hickmann, Maya & Hendriks, Henriëtte. 1999. "Cohesion and Anaphor in Children's Narratives: A Comparison of English, French, German, and Mandarin Chinese". *Journal of Child Language* 26.419–452.

Jin, Lixian, Rogayah A Razak & Lim Oh, Bee. 2012. "C-LARSP: Developing a Chinese Grammatical Profile for Clinical Assessment in Malaysia". *Assessing Grammar: The Languages of LARSP* ed by Martin J. Ball, David Crystal and Paul Fletcher, 208–229. Bristol: Multi-lingual Matters

Justice, Laura M. & Chris, Lankford. 2002. "Preschool Children's Visual Attention to Print during Storybook Reading: Pilot Findings". *Communication Disorders Quarterly* 24.11–21.

Kyratzis, Amy & Guo, Jiansheng. 2001. "Preschool Girls' and Boys' Verbal Conflict Strategies in the United States and China". *Research on Language and Social Interaction* 34:1.45–74.

Labov, William. ed. 1972. *Language in the Inner City: Studies in the Black English Vernacular*. Philadelphia: University of Philadelphia Press.

Li Wei 2010. BAMFLA: Issues, Methods and Directions. A special issue of *International Journal of Bilingualism 14*.

Morton, Helen. 1996. *Becoming Tongan: An Ethnography of Childhood*. Honolulu: University of Hawai'i Press.

Ochs, Elinor. 1988. *Culture and Development: Language Acquisition and Language Socialisation in a Samoan Village*. Cambridge: Cambridge University Press.

Paugh, Amy. 2012. "Local Theories of Child Rearing". *The Handbook of Language Socialisation* ed. by Alessandro Duranti, Elinor Ochs & Bambi B. Schieffelin, 150–168. Malden, MA: Wiley-Blackwell.

Pye, Clifton. 1986. "Quiché Mayan Speech to Children". *Journal of Child Language* 13.85–100.

Ratner, Nan Bernstein & Pye, Clifton. 1984. "Higher Pitch in BT is not Universal: Acoustic Evidence from Quiche Mayan". *Journal of Child Language* 11.515–522.

Schieffelin, Bambi & Ochs, Elinor, eds. 1986. *Language Socialisation across Cultures*. Cambridge: Cambridge University Press.

Shatz, Marilyn. 1991. "Using Cross-cultural Research to Inform us about the Role of Language in Development: Comparisons of Japanese, Korean, and English, and of German, American English, and British English". *Cultural Approaches to Parenting*, ed. by Marc H. Bornstein, 139–153. Hillsdale, NJ: Lawrence Erlbaum Associates.

Snow, Catherine. 1995. "Issues in the Study of Input: Finetuning, Universality, Individual and Developmental Differences, and Necessary Causes". *The Handbook of Child Language* ed. by Paul Fletcher & Brian MacWhinney, 180–193. Oxford: Blackwell.

Stokes, Stephanie F. & Fletcher, Paul. 2000. "Lexical Diversity and Productivity in Cantonese-speaking Children with Specific Language Impairment". *International Journal of Language and Communication Disorders* 35.527–41.

Stokes, Stephanie F. & Fletcher, Paul. 2003. "Aspect Markers in Cantonese-speaking Children with Specific Language Impairment". *Linguistics* 41.381–406.

Veneziano, Edy. 2010. "Conversation in Language Development and Use". *A special issue of First Language* 30.3–4.

Vigil, Debra C. 2002. "Cultural Variations in Attention Regulation: A Comparative Analysis of British and Chinese-immigrant Populations". *International Journal of Language & Communication Disorders* 37.433–458.

Yip, Virginia & Matthews, Stephen. 2007. *The Bilingual Child: Early Development and Language Contact*. Cambridge: Cambridge University Press.

Zhou, Jing. 2002. *The Pragmatic Development of Chinese Children: From 14 months to 32 months*. Nanjing: Nanjing Normal University Press.

Zhou Jing 2009. *Research on Language development of Chinese-speaking Children: Application and Development of CHILDES*. Beijing: Educational Science Publishing House.

Zhou, Jing, Lixian Jin, Jiaru Zhang & Chen, Lili. eds. 2010. *Language Studies of Chinese-speaking Children*. Nanjing: Nanjing Normal University Press.

Zhu Hua 2002. *Phonological Development in Specific Contexts: Studies of Chinese-speaking Children*. Clevedon: Multilingual Matters.

Zhu Hua & Wei, Li. 2008. "Cross-linguistic and Multilingual Perspective on Communicative Competence and Communication Impairment: Pragmatics, Discourse and Sociolinguistics." *Handbook of Clinical Linguistics* ed. by Martin Ball, Michael R. Perkins Nicole Muller & Sara Howard, 146–162. Oxford: Blackwell.

The pragmatic function of self/other reference in Mandarin child language

Chiung-chih Huang
National Chengchi University

This study investigated self/other reference in Mandarin child language by testing the hypothesis that children's overt self/other reference is related to the pragmatic notion of social control (Budwig, 1989, 1990, 1995). The participants were two Mandarin-speaking children and their mothers. Natural mother–child conversations were video-recorded when the children were between the ages of 2;2 and 3;1. Each child and maternal utterance with an implicit or explicit self/other reference was categorized by function as either control act or assertive. The analysis showed that the children tended to use overt forms for self/other reference in control acts while using null forms in assertives. In contrast, the mothers' speech did not reflect such a distinction. The results suggest that social control appears to be a salient notion to Mandarin-speaking children, and that the children organize their use of self/other reference forms around the pragmatic notion of social control.

1.   Introduction

It is well-known that Mandarin permits omitted arguments. In Mandarin, overt reference forms can be omitted provided that the referent can be understood from the context. That is, Mandarin is a null argument language that allows argument omission governed by discourse-pragmatic factors (Huang, 1994, 2000; Li & Thompson, 1981, Tsao, 1990). As seen in Excerpt 1, the subject in Lin's utterance is not specified because the referent is understood from having been mentioned in the preceding utterance.

> Excerpt 1: Lin 2 (2;6)
> *MOT: 達達　在　做　什麼?
>   Dada　zai　zuo shenme
>   (name) PRO do　what
>   'What is Dada doing?'

*LIN: Ø 講　　故事.
　　　　Ø jiang gushi
　　　　　speak story
　　　　'(He is) telling a story.'

It is commonly argued that reference forms for referring to the speaker and the addressee are most readily omitted in Mandarin because they are easily retrievable from the physical interactional context and are always active in discourse, as seen in Excerpt 2.

　　　　Excerpt 2: Jie 3 (2;10)
*MOT: 現在　　Ø 要　　學　　什麼?
　　　　xianzai Ø yao   xue   shenme
　　　　now　　　want learn what
　　　　'What do (you) want to learn now?'

*JIE: Ø 學　　這個 [% pointing at a book].
　　　　Ø xue   zhe-ge
　　　　　learn this
　　　　'(I want) to learn this.'

If Mandarin permits omitted reference forms, an interesting question would be why Mandarin-speaking children and parents sometimes do supply an overt reference form when the referent is understood. Given the availability of physical and discourse contexts to disambiguate implicit self-reference and other-reference, the purpose of this study is to investigate what might provide the impetus for Mandarin-speaking children and their mothers to attempt overt reference to the self and to the addressee.

1.1　Forms and functions of self/other reference

Previous studies have demonstrated that young children use multiple linguistic forms for self/other reference. The seemingly interchangeable use of reference forms in child language has been shown to be related to semantic or pragmatic patterns. Imbens-Baily and Pan (1998) investigated the pragmatics of self/other reference in young children. The study examined self/other reference and communicative intents expressed by children and parents in dyadic interaction at 14, 20 and 32 months. Research questions included whether children's early use of self/other reference pronouns occurred for expression of particular communicative intents, how use changed with age, and whether parent and child pragmatic expressions of self and other were similar. The results showed that the children's early explicit reference to self was used primarily in making statements about their intended actions, in making requests or proposals to their parents and in stating propositions about the world around them. The children during this developmental period were only beginning to refer to the present other and such instances occurred primarily in making requests or proposals. In the communicative contexts in which they explicitly referred to self and other, the children did not appear to exclusively mirror those which were observed in parental speech.

While Imbens-Baily and Pan (1998) studied both self-reference and other-reference in child language, most of the other related studies focused mainly on self-reference. From semantic and pragmatic perspectives, Budwig (1989, 1990, 1995) investigated the relationship between children's use of self-reference forms and the notions of agentivity and control. The children participating in the study ranged between 1;8 and 2;8 at the onset of the study, and they were observed for a four-month period. Budwig divided the children into two groups: *ego-anchored* and *non-ego-anchored*. Ego-anchored children referred primarily to self, using several self-reference forms in the subject position. They tended to use *I* as 'experiencer' of states and actions ranking low in agency, and *Me* as 'volitional agent' of assertions and in control acts such as directives, requests, and protests. Non-ego-anchored children referred to both self and other, and used mainly *I* to refer to self. They often used *I*, *We*, and *My* in utterances ranking low in agentivity or assertions. The results showed that the children's use of self-reference forms was linked to distinct semantic or pragmatic functions, and that they used the first person pronominal forms as markers of various degrees of agentivity and control.

Similar results were observed in Brigaudiot, Morgenstern, and Nicolas (1996). Brigaudiot, et al. analyzed self-reference terms in longitudinal data of two French-speaking children and one English-speaking child between the ages of 1;08 and 2;10. The results showed that the children also employed a contrasted use of self-reference terms in relation to two categories of uses: one corresponding to internal states found in assertions and the other to high agentivity.

Gerhart (1988) also reported different kinds of first-person involvement in child language. The study analyzed the verb morphology and forms of self-reference in a one-year-old's speech (1;10,16 to 2;0,2). It was found that the proper name was used for highly scripted events in which the child was the locus of others' action, and *I* was used when the child was an agent of change or experiencer of desire.

In addition, Smiley and Johnson (2006) explored 2-year-olds' developing self-conceptions by examining the children's uses of self-referring forms to mark contexts that varied in transitivity. It was found that children used self-referring terms systematically in relation to events that varied in transitivity, depending on their preferred terms for self reference (*I* vs. proper name/*me*). 'I-users', children who preferred the first-person pronoun *I* for self-reference, produced relatively more verbs for highly transitive events; 'Name-users', children who preferred their proper names for self-reference, produced relatively more verbs for intransitive events.

As seen in the studies reviewed above, children partition their experiences and create their own form-function mappings. They systematically employ different self/other reference forms to mark these distinct experiences, even though adults may not use language precisely in these ways (Budwig, 2000, Smiley & Johnson, 2006).

1.2 Self/other reference in child Mandarin

As for Mandarin-speaking children, several studies have documented the chronological development of person reference in child Mandarin (Hsu, 1996; Qi, di Biase, & Campbell, 2006; Xu & Min, 1992); in addition, Mandarin-speaking children's use of different self-reference forms was also examined (Chang, 1997).

Xu and Min (1992) showed that Mandarin-speaking children acquired personal pronouns in the order of first person, second person and third person. When the first person pronoun initially appeared at about 1;6, it appeared mostly in subject and possessive positions. Between 1;11 and 2;0, the children produced correct first and second person pronouns in object positions, and at 2;4, correct second person pronouns in subject positions. From 2;7 to 3;0, the children started using the third person pronoun to refer to people but still showed errors before reaching 3;3. In addition, the authors also pointed out that the first person pronoun initially only appeared in certain circumstances such as when the children were 'asking for something'; however, no explanation was provided for this phenomenon. Similarly, Hsu (1996) also reported that Mandarin-speaking children acquired personal pronouns in the order of first person, second person and third person. The first person singular pronoun *wo* emerged at the age of 1;10; the second person singular pronoun *ni* around the age of 2;0, and the third person singular pronoun *ta* around the age of 2;1. Qi, et al. (2006) investigated the development from nominal to pronominal person reference in a Mandarin-English bilingual child between 1;7 and 4;0. It was observed that the bilingual child's emergence of person reference experienced three developmental phases: (1) kinship terms and lack of self-reference (1;7–2;0); (2) nominal reference to self and others (2;0–3;0,7), and (3) emergence of first person pronominal reference alongside other self-reference expressions (3;0,7–4;0). The study showed that in bilingual L1 acquisition, first and second person pronominal reference can emerge significantly later than in monolingual L1 acquisition.

Chang (1997), on the other hand, focused on Mandarin-speaking children's use of different self-reference forms around 2;0 to 3;0. Three self-reference forms were examined: NULL, NAME (the deviant nominal form), and WO (the first person pronoun). To investigate the factors which contributed to the children's usages of the different forms, Chang explored three proposals: Bloom's (1990) VP length hypothesis, Budwig's (1989) semantic hypothesis, and Budwig's (1989) pragmatic hypothesis. The VP length hypothesis suggests that children's subject-less sentences tend to have longer VPs than sentences with subjects. The semantic hypothesis assumes that children's choice between different forms of self-reference is related to the level of agentivity. The pragmatic hypothesis assumes that the pragmatic function of the utterance — whether it is an assertive or a control act — can account for children's choice of self-reference forms. The results showed that the VP length hypothesis failed to explain the children's choice of self-reference forms. Instead, the patterns of children's self-reference forms were in accordance with Budwig's semantic and pragmatic hypotheses. That is, at the semantic level, NAME was associated with utterances high in agentivity; at the pragmatic level, WO was associated with control utterances.

1.3 The present study

The purpose of the present study is to explore the pragmatic functions of Mandarin-speaking children's use of self/other reference forms in mother–child interaction. As seen in Budwig (1989, 1990, 1995) and Chang (1997), the pragmatic distinction involving social control appears to play an important role in children's choice of different self-reference forms. This study attempted to investigate whether the notion of social control could be used to explain not only children's use of self-reference forms but also their use of other-reference forms. In addition, while Budwig and Chang focused on children's use of different overt forms, this study analyzed Mandarin-speaking children's choices between null forms and overt forms. As stated above, null forms are important devices for self/other reference in Mandarin conversation. The study thus explored Mandarin-speaking children's self/other reference by testing the hypothesis that children's overt self/other reference is related to the pragmatic notion of social control. In order to better understand self/other reference in Mandarin child language, the mothers' speech was also examined for comparison.

2. Methods

2.1 Participants and data

The participants in this study were two Mandarin-speaking children and their mothers, who lived in the northern part of Taiwan. The two children, Lin and Jie (pseudonyms), were both girls. Both of the mothers, as well as the fathers, had received post-graduate education. The data used in this study consisted of eight hours of natural mother–child conversation video-recorded at the participants' homes, with four one-hour sessions with each dyad. Lin and her mother's data were recorded when the child was at the ages of 2;2, 2;6, 2:10 and 3;1, and Jie and her mother's data were recorded when the child was at the ages of 2;2, 2;7, 2;10 and 3;1. Figure 1 shows the mean length of utterance (MLU, defined in terms of average number of words per utterance) of the children's language at the time of each data session.

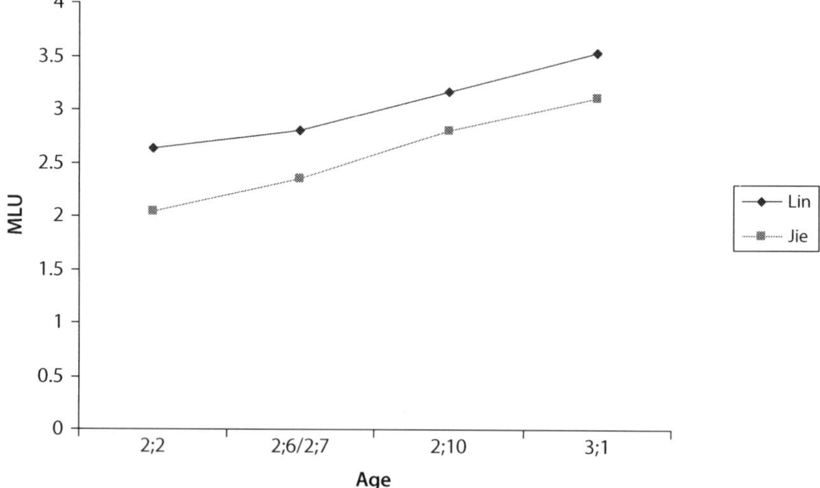

Figure 1. The MLU at each data session

As seen in the figure, both of the children's MLU became longer with age. However, while the children were about the same age at the time of each data session, Lin's MLU was longer than Jie's at every session. It appeared that Lin's language development was slightly more advanced than that of Jie's during the data collection period.

All of the data were collected in the living rooms of the two homes, and the two dyads were involved in similar activities during the data sessions, such as eating, reading books, and playing with toys. Other family members also occasionally participated in the interactions. The data collected were transcribed following the CHAT conventions and were analyzed using the CLAN program (MacWhinney, 2000).

2.2 Analytical framework

Every child utterance in the data with an implicit or explicit self/other-reference form was included for analysis. In order to compare the children's use of self/other-reference with that of the mothers, half an hour of data from each of the one-hour sessions were further analyzed to examine the mothers' speech. Both child utterances and maternal utterances were coded for reference forms and pragmatic functions.

1. Reference forms
Each child and maternal utterance with self/other reference was analyzed in terms of whether an explicit reference form was used.

a. Null form: Absence of an explicit form
b. Overt form: An explicit reference form is used, including pronominal (e.g., *wo* 'I', *ni* 'you') and nominal forms (e.g., proper names, kinship terms).

2. Pragmatic functions
Child and maternal utterances which involved self/other reference were further analyzed in terms of the notion of social control. A general distinction was drawn between utterances which functioned as control acts and those which functioned as assertives (Budwig, 1989, 1995).

a. Control act: The utterance brings about a change in the environment, and the notion of control is central. (e.g., requests, warnings, and commands).
b. Assertive: The utterance represents an existing state, and control is not at issue (e.g., statements).

Excerpt 3 demonstrates an example of a control act. In this excerpt Lin's utterance in Line 1 functioned as a control act, in which the child requested the mother to read a story for her. As seen in the utterance, the overt other-reference form *ni* 'you' was used by the child.

     Excerpt 3: Lin 2 (2;6)
*LIN: 你　講　　這　個 [% giving the mother a book] . ←
       ni　jiang　zhe　ge
       2SG speak this CL
       'You read this (story).'
*MOT: 好 .
       hao
       alright
       'Alright.'

Excerpt 4 is another example of a control act. In this example, Jie asked the mother to bring her some water, and the mother responded to the child's request by giving her a glass of water. The child used the overt self-reference form *wo* 'I' in the utterance.

Excerpt 4: Jie 3 (2;10)
*JIE: 我　要　喝　水.   ←
wo yao he   shui
1sg want drink water
'I want to drink water.'
*MOT: 0 [% giving the child a glass of water]

Excerpt 5 demonstrates an example of an assertive. In this excerpt, the mother and the child were engaged in a pretend play. The child's statement in Line 3 functioned as an assertive, in which the child used a null form for self-reference.

Excerpt 5: Lin 3 (2;10)
*MOT: 我　什麼　時候　可以　吃到　你　做　的
wo shenme shihou keyi chi-dao ni   zuo   de
1sg what   time   can   eat-arrive you make nom

好吃　的　餅乾?
haochi de   binggan
tasty   assoc cookie
'When can I try some of the tasty cookies that you make?'

*LIN: 等　一下 -:.
deng yixia
wait a while
'Just a second.'
*LIN: Ø 現在　在　做　早餐　啦! ←
Ø xianzai zai zuo   zaocan   la
    now   pro make breakfast prt
'(I) am fixing breakfast now.'

Excerpt 6 illustrates another case of an assertive. As seen in Line 2, the child's utterance represented an existing state and functioned as an assertive. The overt self-reference form *wo* 'I' was used in the assertive.

Excerpt 6: Jie 1 (2;2)
*MOT: Jie   你　有沒有   錢錢?
Jie   ni   you-mei-you   qianqian
(Name) 2sg have-not-have money
'Jie, do you have any money?'

*JIE: 我　沒有　　錢錢.　　　　←
         wo mei-you qianqian
         1SG not-have money
         'I don't have money.'

3. Results

3.1 Instances of self/other reference

Table 1 presents the number of instances of self-reference and other-reference in the children's speech. As seen in the table, the children referred to self much more frequently than referring to other in all of the sessions. Overall, Lin used more than three times as many self-reference tokens as other-reference tokens while Jie used more than five times as many self-reference tokens as other-reference ones. In other words, the children talked more about themselves than about their mothers.

Table 2 presents the number of instances of self-reference and other-reference in the mothers' speech. In contrast to the patterns observed in the children's speech, the mothers referred to other much more frequently than referring to self in every session. Overall, both Lin's mother and Jie's each used more than three times as many other-reference tokens as self-reference tokens. In other words, the mothers talked more about the children than about themselves. Tables 1 and 2 thus show that the focus in the mother–child interactions was talking about the children rather than about the mothers.

Table 1. Number of instances of self-reference and other-reference in the children's speech

	Self-reference	Other-reference
Lin 1	89	24
Lin 2	152	68
Lin 3	63	19
Lin 4	98	20
Total	402	131
Jie 1	131	11
Jie 2	112	13
Jie 3	155	58
Jie 4	224	28
Total	622	110

Table 2. Number of instances of self-reference and other-reference in the mothers' speech

	Self-reference	Other-reference
LinM 1	69	234
LinM 2	62	191
LinM 3	45	187
LinM 4	48	188
Total	224	800
JieM 1	104	344
JieM 2	76	268
JieM 3	83	308
JieM 4	95	270
Total	358	1190

3.2 Forms and functions of self-reference

Self-reference in the children's and the mothers' speech was examined in terms of the reference forms used. In addition, the relationship between self-reference forms and pragmatic functions was also analyzed.

3.2.1 *Children's speech*

Table 3 demonstrates the number and proportion of null forms and overt forms used by the two children for self-reference. In Lin's speech, the proportions of null forms ranged from 31.75% to 55.10% across the four sessions, and the proportions of overt forms ranged from 44.90% to 68.25%. The proportions of null forms and overt forms used in each session did not differ significantly except in the session of Lin 3, in which overt forms were used significantly more frequently than null forms ($p < .05$). Overall, the proportions of null forms and overt forms did not show a significant difference, suggesting that Lin used overt forms and null forms with a similar frequency when referring to self.

As for Jie's speech, similar patterns were observed. The proportions of null forms ranged from 37.42% to 57.25% across the four sessions, and the proportions of overt forms ranged from 42.75% to 62.58%. The proportions of null forms and overt forms used in each session did not differ significantly except in the session of Jie 3, in which overt forms was used significantly more frequently than null forms ($p < .05$). Overall, the proportions of null forms and overt forms used by Jie did not show a significant difference, suggesting that Jie also used overt forms and null forms with a similar frequency for self-reference.

Table 3. Distributions of self-reference forms used by the two children

Self- reference	Null		Overt		Total	
	N	%	N	%	N	%
Lin 1	43	48.31	46	51.69	89	100
Lin 2	60	39.47	92	60.53	152	100
Lin 3	20	31.75	43	68.25	63	100
Lin 4	54	55.10	44	44.90	98	100
Total	177	44.03	225	55.97	402	100
Jie 1	75	57.25	56	42.75	131	100
Jie 2	47	41.96	65	58.04	112	100
Jie 3	58	37.42	97	62.58	155	100
Jie 4	116	51.79	108	48.21	224	100
Total	296	47.59	326	52.41	622	100

Further analysis was conducted to examine the relationship between the children's use of self-reference forms and pragmatic functions. Table 4 displays the distributions of null forms and overt forms used by the children with respect to the functions of control acts and assertives in each session.

As seen in Table 4, the distributions of self-reference forms in control acts and in assertives revealed very different patterns in the children's speech. Lin used a high rate of overt forms in control acts; the percentage of overt forms became much lower in assertives. Take the session of Lin 2 for example. Overt forms were used 83.53% of the time in control acts but only 31.34% of the time in assertives. In contrast, Lin used a high rate of null forms in assertives, and she used null forms much less frequently in control acts. For example, null forms were used 68.66% of the time in assertives and 16.47% of the time in control acts in the session of Lin 2. Such distribution patterns were observed in all of the sessions. Chi-square analyses showed that Lin's use of the two types of self-reference forms was significantly different in relation to the pragmatic functions in each of the data sessions. The results thus revealed that Lin's use of self-reference forms was affected by the notion of social control.

Similar distribution patterns and statistical results were also observed in Jie's speech. Jie also used overt forms significantly more frequently in control acts than in assertives, and null forms significantly more frequently in assertives than in control acts. As seen in Table 4, the results of the Chi-square analyses indicated a statistical significance in each session except in the session of Jie 1.

The results of Table 4 thus revealed that the use of self-reference forms by both of the children was influenced by the pragmatic notion of social control. Both of

Table 4. Distributions of self-reference forms with respect to pragmatic functions in the children's data

Self-reference		Control acts		Assertives		χ^2
		N	%	N	%	
Lin 1	Null	19	36.54	24	64.86	6.95**
	Overt	33	63.46	13	35.14	
	Total	52	100	37	100	
Lin 2	Null	14	16.47	46	68.66	42.71***
	Overt	71	83.53	21	31.34	
	Total	85	100	67	100	
Lin 3	Null	9	22.50	11	47.83	4.32*
	Overt	31	77.50	12	52.17	
	Total	40	100	23	100	
Lin 4	Null	16	34.78	38	73.08	14.47***
	Overt	30	65.22	14	26.93	
	Total	46	100	52	100	
Jie 1	Null	34	51.52	41	63.08	*n.s.*
	Overt	32	48.48	24	36.93	
	Total	66	100	65	100	
Jie 2	Null	24	32.88	23	58.97	7.11**
	Overt	49	67.12	16	41.03	
	Total	73	100	39	100	
Jie 3	Null	27	26.21	31	59.62	16.46***
	Overt	76	73.79	21	40.38	
	Total	103	100	52	100	
Jie 4	Null	30	30.93	86	67.72	29.81***
	Overt	67	69.07	41	32.29	
	Total	97	100	127	100	

*$p < .05$; **$p < .01$; ***$p < .001$
n.s.: not significant

them tended to use overt forms for self-reference in control acts and null forms in assertives.

3.2.2 *Mothers' speech*

Table 5 demonstrates the number and proportion of null forms and overt forms used by the two mothers for self-reference. In the speech of Lin's mother, the proportions of null forms ranged from 10.42% to 25.81% across the four sessions, and the proportions of overt forms ranged from 74.19% to 89.58%. The proportions of null forms and overt forms used in each session differed significantly ($p < .05$): Overt forms were used significantly more frequently than null forms. Overall, Lin's mother used null forms 16.07% of the time and overt forms 83.93% of the time when referring to self.

Similar distribution patterns were observed in the speech of Jie's mother. The proportions of null forms ranged from 10.53% to 18.27% across the four sessions, and the proportions of overt forms ranged from 81.73% to 89.47%. Overt forms were used significantly more frequently than null forms by Jie's mother in each data session. Overall, Jie's mother used null forms 13.97% of the time and overt forms 86.03% of the time for self-reference.

Comparing the results shown in Tables 5 and 3, we observed that while the children used null forms and overt forms with similar frequency for self-reference, the mothers used null forms less frequently than overt forms. The results showed that the children relied more heavily on null forms for self-reference than the mothers.

Further analysis was conducted to examine the relationship between the mothers' use of self-reference forms and pragmatic functions. Table 6 presents the distributions of null forms and overt forms used by the mothers with respect to the functions of control acts and assertives in each of the data sessions.

Table 6 shows that the distributions of self-reference forms in control acts and in assertives revealed similar patterns of use in the mothers' speech. Lin's mother used overt forms more frequently than null forms in control acts as well as in

Table 5. Distributions of self-reference forms used by the two mothers

Self-reference	Null		Overt		Total	
	N	%	N	%	N	%
LinM 1	8	11.59	61	88.41	69	100
LinM 2	16	25.81	46	74.19	62	100
LinM 3	7	15.56	38	84.44	45	100
LinM 4	5	10.42	43	89.58	48	100
Total	36	16.07	188	83.93	224	100
JieM 1	19	18.27	85	81.73	104	100
JieM 2	8	10.53	68	89.47	76	100
JieM 3	11	13.25	72	86.75	83	100
JieM 4	12	12.63	83	87.37	95	100
Total	50	13.97	308	86.03	358	100

assertives in each data session. The Chi-square analyses showed that the distribution of self-reference forms in control acts did not differ significantly from that in assertives in any of the sessions except in the session of LinM 3, in which the result reached a significance ($\chi2(1) = 4.80$, $p < .05$).

Similar distribution patterns and statistical results were also observed in the speech of Jie's mother. As seen in Table 6, Jie's mother used overt forms more frequently than null forms in control acts as well as in assertives. The Chi-square

Table 6. Distributions of self-reference forms with respect to pragmatic functions in the mothers' data

Self-reference		Control acts		Assertives		$\chi2$
		N	%	N	%	
LinM 1	Null	5	8.93	3	23.08	*n.s.*
	Overt	51	91.07	10	76.92	
	Total	56	100	13	100	
LinM 2	Null	11	22.45	3	23.08	*n.s.*
	Overt	38	77.55	10	76.92	
	Total	49	100	13	100	
LinM 3	Null	3	8.82	4	36.36	4.80*
	Overt	31	91.18	7	63.64	
	Total	34	100	11	100	
LinM 4	Null	4	14.29	2	10	*n.s.*
	Overt	24	85.71	18	90	
	Total	28	100	20	100	
JieM 1	Null	11	14.67	8	27.59	*n.s.*
	Overt	64	85.33	21	72.41	
	Total	75	100	29	100	
JieM 2	Null	1	2.78	6	15	*n.s.*
	Overt	35	97.22	34	85	
	Total	36	100	40	100	
JieM 3	Null	8	11.94	2	12.5	*n.s.*
	Overt	59	88.06	14	87.5	
	Total	67	100	16	100	
JieM 4	Null	7	11.67	5	14.29	*n.s.*
	Overt	53	88.33	30	85.71	
	Total	60	100	35	100	

*$p < .05$
n.s.: not significant

analyses showed that the distributions of self-reference forms did not differ significantly with regard to the pragmatic functions in any of the data sessions. The results thus suggested that the mothers' choices of self-reference forms were not influenced by the pragmatic distinction between control acts and assertives.

3.3 Forms and functions of other-reference

The distributions of other-reference forms in the children's and the mothers' speech were also examined. In addition, other-reference forms were further analyzed in relation to pragmatic functions.

3.3.1 *Children's speech*

Table 7 demonstrates the number and proportion of null forms and overt forms used by the two children for other-reference. In Lin's speech, the proportions of null forms ranged from 7.35% to 15.79% across the four sessions, and the proportions of overt forms ranged from 84.21% to 92.65%. The proportions of null forms and overt forms used in each session differed significantly ($p < .05$): Lin used significantly more overt forms than null forms for other-reference in every session. Overall, Lin used null forms 10.69% of the time and overt forms 89.31% of the time when referring to other.

As for Jie's speech, the proportions of null forms ranged from 15.52% to 46.15% across the four sessions, and the proportions of overt forms ranged from 53.85% to 84.48%. Overt forms were used significantly more frequently than null forms by Jie in each data session for other-reference ($p < .05$) except in the session of Jie 2, in which the two types of reference forms were used with similar frequency. Overall, Jie used null forms 21.82% of the time and overt forms 78.18% of the time when referring to other.

Further analysis was conducted to examine the relationship between the children's use of other-reference forms and pragmatic functions. Table 8 shows the distributions of null forms and overt forms used by the children with respect to the functions of control acts and assertives in each of the data sessions.

The analysis of each session revealed that the children's other-reference occurred mainly in control acts. Since most of the sessions contained only a small number of instances of other-reference in assertives, the distributions of other-reference forms in assertives shown in the table may not represent a true picture of the distribution. In addition, it was not appropriate to carry out a Chi-square analysis to examine the distributions in any of the sessions due to the limited number of tokens of other-reference in assertives.

As stated above, it was not appropriate to use a Chi-square test for each session because of the limited number of tokens of other-reference in assertives. A

Table 7. Distributions of other-reference forms used by the two children

Other-reference	Null		Overt		Total	
	N	%	N	%	N	%
Lin 1	3	12.50	21	87.50	24	100
Lin 2	5	7.35	63	92.65	68	100
Lin 3	3	15.79	16	84.21	19	100
Lin 4	3	15.00	17	85.00	20	100
Total	14	10.69	117	89.31	131	100
Jie 1	2	18.18	9	81.82	11	100
Jie 2	6	46.15	7	53.85	13	100
Jie 3	9	15.52	49	84.48	58	100
Jie 4	7	25.00	21	75.00	28	100
Total	24	21.82	86	78.18	110	100

Chi-square analysis was thus conducted based on the collapsed dataset across the children and the sessions in order to obtain a general picture of the children's use of other-reference forms with regard to the pragmatic functions. The results are shown in Table 9.

As seen in Table 9, the results indicated that the distributions of null forms and overt forms for other-reference differed significantly in control acts and in assertives $(\chi2(1)=4.18,\ p<.05)$. The children used overt forms significantly more frequently in control acts than in assertives (86.53% > 72.73%) and they used null forms significantly less frequently in control acts than in assertives (13.47% < 27.27%). The results suggested that the children's use of other-reference forms was also influenced by the notion of social control.

3.3.2   *Mothers' speech*

Table 10 demonstrates the number and proportion of null forms and overt forms used by the two mothers for other-reference. In the speech of Lin's mother, the proportions of null forms ranged from 38.22% to 46.15% across the four sessions, and the proportions of overt forms ranged from 53.85% to 61.78%. Overall, Lin's mother used null forms 43.25% of the time and overt forms 56.75% of the time when referring to other. As for the speech of Jie's mother, the proportions of null forms ranged from 35.19% to 43.61% across the four sessions, and the proportions of overt forms ranged from 56.39% to 64.81%. Overall, Jie's mother used null forms 40.42% of the time and overt forms 59.58% of the time for other-reference. Comparing the results in Tables 10 and 7, we observed that the mothers used null forms more frequently than the children for other-reference.

Table 8. Distributions of other-reference forms with respect to pragmatic functions in the children's data

Other-reference		Control acts		Assertives		χ^2
		N	%	N	%	
Lin 1	Null	2	9.09	1	50	NA
	Overt	20	90.91	1	50	
	Total	22	100	2	100	
Lin 2	Null	4	6.25	1	25	NA
	Overt	60	93.75	3	75	
	Total	64	100	4	100	
Lin 3	Null	3	16.67	0	0	NA
	Overt	15	83.33	1	100	
	Total	18	100	1	100	
Lin 4	Null	3	16.67	0	0	NA
	Overt	15	83.33	2	100	
	Total	18	100	2	100	
Jie 1	Null	1	33.33	1	12.5	NA
	Overt	2	66.67	7	87.5	
	Total	3	100	8	100	
Jie 2	Null	6	50	0	0	NA
	Overt	6	50	1	100	
	Total	12	100	1	100	
Jie 3	Null	7	12.73	2	66.67	NA
	Overt	48	87.27	1	33.33	
	Total	55	100	3	100	
Jie 4	Null	3	18.75	4	33.33	NA
	Overt	13	81.25	8	66.67	
	Total	16	100	12	100	

NA: not applicable

Table 9. Distributions of other-reference forms with respect to pragmatic functions in the collapsed child data

Other-reference	Control acts		Assertives		χ^2
	N	%	N	%	
Null	28	13.47%	9	27.27%	4.18*
Overt	180	86.53%	24	72.73%	
Total	208	100	33	100	

*$p < .05$

Table 10. Distributions of other-reference forms used by the two mothers

Other-reference	Null		Overt		Total	
	N	%	N	%	N	%
LinM 1	108	46.15	126	53.85	234	100
LinM 2	73	38.22	118	61.78	191	100
LinM 3	86	45.99	101	54.01	187	100
LinM 4	79	42.02	109	57.98	188	100
Total	346	43.25	454	56.75	800	100
JieM 1	150	43.61	194	56.39	344	100
JieM 2	107	39.93	161	60.07	268	100
JieM 3	129	41.88	179	58.12	308	100
JieM 4	95	35.19	175	64.81	270	100
Total	481	40.42	709	59.58	1190	100

Further analysis was conducted to examine the relationship between the mothers' use of other-reference forms and pragmatic functions. Table 11 displays the results.

Table 11 demonstrates that the distributions of other-reference forms in control acts and in assertives revealed similar patterns in the mothers' speech. In the speech of Lin's mother, the distributions did not differ significantly in any session. Similarly, in the speech of Jie's mother, the results also did not reach statistical significance in any session except in the session of JieM 3 ($\chi2(1)=6.81$, $p<.01$). It appeared that the mothers' use of other-reference forms was not affected by the distinction between control acts and assertives.

4.   Discussion and Conclusion

The results of this study have shown that the distributions of null forms and overt forms in the children's speech differed significantly in control acts and in assertives for both self-reference and other-reference. That is, the children tended to use overt forms for self/other reference in control acts while using null forms in assertives. In contrast, the analysis of the mothers' speech showed that the mothers' use of self/other reference forms did not reflect such a distinction. The results suggested that social control appears to be a salient notion to Mandarin-speaking children, and that children organize their use of self/other reference forms around the pragmatic notion of social control. The findings of this study are consistent with those reported in Budwig (1989, 1995) and Chang (1997). However, while Budwig and

Table 11. Distributions of other-reference forms with respect to pragmatic functions in the mothers' data

Other-reference		Control acts		Assertives		χ^2
		N	%	N	%	
LinM 1	Null	95	48.72	14	35.9	*n.s.*
	Overt	100	51.28	25	64.1	
	Total	195	100	39	100	
LinM 2	Null	67	38.95	6	31.58	*n.s.*
	Overt	105	61.05	13	68.42	
	Total	172	100	19	100	
LinM 3	Null	85	48.3	2	18.18	*n.s.*
	Overt	91	51.7	9	81.82	
	Total	176	100	11	100	
LinM 4	Null	72	43.37	7	31.82	*n.s.*
	Overt	94	56.63	15	68.18	
	Total	166	100	22	100	
JieM 1	Null	126	43	23	45.1	*n.s.*
	Overt	167	57	28	54.9	
	Total	293	100	51	100	
JieM 2	Null	95	40.77	10	28.57	*n.s.*
	Overt	138	59.22	25	71.43	
	Total	233	100	35	100	
JieM 3	Null	114	45.78	16	27.12	6.81**
	Overt	135	54.22	43	72.88	
	Total	249	100	59	100	
JieM 4	Null	78	37.32	16	26.23	*n.s.*
	Overt	131	62.68	45	73.77	
	Total	209	100	61	100	

**p < .01
n.s.: not significant

Chang focused on the analysis of self-reference, this study revealed that the use of both self-reference forms and other-reference forms in child Mandarin was related to the pragmatic notion of social control.

Slobin (1981, 1985) has suggested that particular 'prototypical events' provide a framework for the early organization of linguistic forms. One of such type of events is referred to as the 'manipulative activity scene', in which "an agent carries out a physical and perceptible change of state in a patient by means of direct body contact or with an instrument under the agent's control" (Slobin, 1985, p. 1175). The notion of agentivity has thus been considered primarily from the standpoint of physical causation. However, as suggested by Budwig (1989, 1995), children might work with a broader prototype of agentivity, and they might integrate their budding notion of social control into the manipulative activity scene. This study showed that Mandarin-speaking children link the use of self/other reference forms with the notion of social control, suggesting that Mandarin-speaking children take social control to be relevant for their organization of linguistic forms. The finding appears to provide a piece of evidence that Mandarin-speaking children integrate pragmatic components into the agentivity scene.

The high concentration of overt self/other reference forms in expressing control acts in the children's speech suggests a rudimentary, implicit understanding of the instrumental function of language to alter the world. The context of social control appears to be fertile ground for the early explicit representation of self. While the children referred to other much less frequently than referring to self, a finding consistent with those in previous studies (e.g., Imbens-Bailey & Pan, 1998), the context of social control also appears to promote the early production of other-reference.

The results also showed that the distribution patterns of self/other reference forms observed in the children's speech were not present in the mother's speech. The finding is consistent with those reported in Imbens-Bailey and Pan (1998) and Budwig (2000), which indicated that in the contexts in which the children in their studies explicitly referred to self and other, they did not appear to exclusively mirror those which were observed in parental speech. It appears that Mandarin-speaking children employ the overt and null forms for self/other-reference to mark distinct pragmatic functions before using these reference forms more conventionally. Further studies are needed to better understand the extent to which children are influenced by the form-function patterns found in input and the extent to which children creatively construct their own form-function mappings during the course of language acquisition.

Furthermore, the longitudinal data (2;2–3;1) analyzed in this study do not appear to reveal clear developmental changes. Chang (1997) suggested that children between 2;0 and 3;0 years of age are at the so-called 'prime phase', and that they use different forms of self-reference with distinctive semantic and pragmatic patterns. Then, later, these distinctions gradually disappear during the transition phase between the prime phase and the adult phase. Since previous studies of children's acquisition of person reference focused mainly on children younger than 3;0, further studies are needed to investigate the speech of older children in order to obtain a clearer picture of the developmental trend of person reference in child language.

References

Bloom, Paul. 1990. "Subjectless sentences in child language". *Linguistic Inquiry* 21.491–504.

Brigaudiot, Mireille, Morgenstern, Aliyah & Catherine, Nicolas. 1996. "'Guillaume i va pas gagner, c'est d'abord maman'": Genesis of the first-person pronoun". *Children's language,* ed. by C. Johnson & J. Gilbert, vol. 9, 105–116. Mahwah, NJ: Lawrence Erlbaum Associates.

Budwig, Nancy. 1989. "The linguistic marking of agentivity and control in child language". *Journal of Child Language* 16.263–284.

Budwig, Nancy. 1990. "The linguistic marking of non-prototypical agency: An exploration into children's use of passives". *Linguistics* 28.1221–1252.

Budwig, Nancy. 1995. *A Developmental-functionalist Approach to Child Language.* Mahawah, New Jersey: Lawrence Erlbaum Associates.

Budwig, Nancy. 2000. "Language and the construction of the self". *Communication: An arena for development,* ed. by N. Budwig, I. C. Uzgiris & J. Wertsch, 195–214. Stamford, CT: Ablex.

Chang, Hsiao-Chih. 1997. *The Acquisition of Chinese First Person Reference.* Ph.D. dissertation. Boston University.

Gerhardt, Julie. 1988. "From discourse to semantics: the development of verb morphology and forms of self-reference in the speech of a two-year-old". *Journal of Child Language* 15.337–393.

Hsu, Joseph H. 1996. *A Study of the Stages of Development and Acquisition of Mandarin Chinese by Children in Taiwan.* Taipei: Crane.

Huang, Yan. 1994. *The Syntax and Pragmatics of Anaphora: A study with special reference to Chinese.* Cambridge: Cambridge University Press.

Huang, Yan. 2000. *Anaphora: A crosslinguistic study.* Oxford: Oxford University Press.

Imbens-Bailey, Alison. & Alexander, Pan. 1998. "The pragmatics of self- and other-reference in young children". *Social Development* 7:2.219–233.

Li, Charles N. & Sandra A, Thompson. 1981. *Mandarin Chinese: A functional reference grammar.* Berkeley, CA: University of California Press.

MacWhinney, Brian, 2000. *The CHILDES Project: Tools for analyzing talk,* 3rd ed. Mahwah, NJ.: Lawrence Erlbaum.

Qi, Ruying, di Biase, Bruno & Stuart, Campbell. 2006. "The transition from nominal to pronominal person reference in the early language of a Mandarin-English bilingual child". *International Journal of Bilingualism* 10:3.301–329.

Slobin, Dan. 1981. "The origins of grammatical encoding of events". *The child's construction of language,* ed. by W. Deutsch. London: Academic Press.

Slobin, Dan. 1985. "Crosslinguistic evidence for the Language Making Capacity". *The crosslinguistic study of language acquisition,* ed. by D. Slobin. Hillsdale NJ: Erlbaum.

Smiley, Patricia A. & Rachel S, Johnson. 2006. "Self-referring terms, event transitivity and development of self". *Cognitive Development* 21.266–284.

Tsao, Feng-fu. 1990. *Sentence and clause structure in Chinese: A function perspective.* Taipei. Student Book.

Xu, Zhengyuan, & Ruifang, Min. 1992. "A study on the acquisition of personal pronouns by Chinese-speaking children". *Acta Psychologica Sinica* 24:4.337–345.

Appendix

Transcription conventions

-:	Previous word lengthened
[% text]	Comments on main line

Gloss abbreviations

1SG	First person singular pronoun
2SG	Second person singular pronoun
ASSOC	Associative
CL	Classifier
PRO	Progressive aspect
NOM	Nominalizer
PRT	Particle

Tense and temporality

How young children express time in Cantonese

Shek Kam Tse, Hui Li and Shing On Leung
The University of Hong Kong / The University of Hong Kong /
University of Macau

This study investigated how a representative sample of 492 Cantonese-speaking children aged 36, 48 and 60 months expressed time during naturalistic conversations with peers. Spontaneous utterances produced by dyads of children in a 30-minute role-play context were collected, transcribed and analyzed. A productive repertoire of 62 nouns, 69 adverbs and 9 aspects was identified and classified into a typology. An age-related increase in types of temporal noun and adverb and repertoire size was found. It was also discovered that three-year-olds might alrcady possess knowledge of aspect markers even though they might not be able to produce temporal nouns about "season" and "week" before 4 or 5 years of age. Some instances of double aspectual marking and misplacing aspects were found in the expressions. Linguistic, cognitive and conversational influences presumed to shape performance are discussed together with the implications of the findings for early childhood language education.

1. Introduction

An understanding of time is a fundamental concept in theories of cognition and communication and has been of central concern in many cross-linguistic studies of language acquisition and cognitive development (Aksu-Koc, 1998; Antinucci & Miller, 1976; Huang, 2003, 2006; Li & Bowerman, 1998; Shirai, Slobin, & Weist, 1998; Weist, Atanassova, Wysocka, & Pawlak, 1999). In learning to understand and express the notion of time, children need to acquire knowledge of tense and aspect, the important elements of most world languages (Li & Shirai, 2000). However, Chinese languages, including Mandarin and Cantonese, are tenseless and do not have morphological markers to indicate tense, gender and plurality (Cao, Li, Yuan, & Wong, 2006; Huang, 2006; Li & Shirai, 2000; Matthews & Yip, 2011). Instead, time and temporal relations are expressed by a combination of aspect markers, temporal adverbials and contextual factors in a relatively free word order (Huang, 2003; Li & Shirai, 2000). Discourse-pragmatic features thus play an important role in meaningful communication in Chinese (Huang, 2006). The complex system of Chinese temporality poses major problems for young children and their language teachers. Many studies of the acquisition of Chinese temporality feature young Mandarin-speaking children with their utterances elicited in contrived settings and via simulations (Erbaugh, 1992; Huang, 2003, 2006; Li, 1990; Li & Bowerman, 1998; Li & Shirai, 2000). Naturalistic methods are needed to track the natural occurrence of tense-aspect forms in young children's Chinese speech (Shirai et al., 1998), especially in the case of early childhood Cantonese, which features a more complicated system of aspect markers than Mandarin (Li & Shirai, 2000; Matthews & Yip, 2011). Although there is a considerable number of studies in the acquisition of Cantonese aspect markers among children with specific language impairment (SLI) (Fletcher, Leonard, Stokes, & Wong, 2005; Luk, 2001; Stokes & Fletcher, 2000, 2003; Wong, Stokes, & Fletcher, 2003), there is a dearth of large-scale studies of the development of temporality in Cantonese-speaking children. The present study aims to understand the developmental routes of temporality in Cantonese-speaking preschoolers by analyzing the largest corpus of early child Cantonese, the Early Child Cantonese Corpus (ECCC) that we established in the past decade (Tse, Chan, Li & Kwong, 2002; Tse, Chan, & Li, 2005; Tse, Li, & Leung, 2007).

1.1   How time is expressed in Chinese languages

Time may be expressed in English by the tense of verbs to indicate when things take place, whereas in Chinese languages verbs do not indicate time, gender or plurality by inflection (Li & Shirai, 2000). Instead, a combination of temporal adverbials, aspect markers and contextual factors are needed to express time and temporal relations (Huang, 2003). For example, in the Cantonese utterance *ji1gaa1 ngo5 doek3 **gan2** nei5go3 BB* (now I am kissing your baby)*, the adverb *ji1gaa1* means *for the time being* while the aspect *gan2* specifies the ongoing status of the action. The non-Chinese speaking reader may be helped by the following paragraphs which summarize expression of time in Cantonese.

Aspectual forms are the most important device for expressing temporality in Chinese languages (Huang, 2003, 2006; Luk, 2001). They exist in monosyllabic bound grammatical forms in Cantonese and occur immediately after predicate verbs or adjectives to convey temporal meaning (Wong et al., 2003). Pragmatically driven in use, an aspect marker serves two functions in daily conversation: (i) it functions as a "situation aspect" (Smith, 1983) or "lexical aspect" (Li & Bowerman, 1998) referring to the temporal meaning inherent in the lexical items describing the situation; and (ii) it functions as a "viewpoint aspect" (Smith, 1983, 1997) or "grammatical aspect" (Li & Bowerman, 1998) encoding the speaker's viewpoint of the temporal contours of the event described in the utterance, whether an event is recently completed or ongoing, or whether it is brief or habitual. Recently, Chen and Shirai (2010) found that the acquisition of aspect marking in Mandarin-speaking children generally follows the predictions of the aspect hypothesis, which tends to support a usage-based learning process in accord with a language-specific system of aspectual semantics. This finding could be examined with Cantonese-speaking children to see whether their language development follows the same pattern.

Aspect markers may be classified into four categories in Mandarin (Li & Bowerman, 1998) and six in Cantonese (Wong et al., 2003):

1. Progressive markers indicate that an action or event is ongoing, with a preverbal *zai4* needed in Mandarin (Li, 1990; Li & Bowerman, 1998; Huang, 2003) and a post-verbal *gan2* used in Cantonese (Luk, 2001; Wong et al., 2003).
2. Durative markers indicate a situation that should be viewed as enduring or continuing, with *zhe* used most frequently with verbs that specify a state in Mandarin, and *zyu6* used in Cantonese (Wong et al., 2003).
3. Perfective markers *le* in Mandarin (Chao, 1968) and *zo2* in Cantonese (Wong et al., 2003) are markers of completion and present the described situation as a whole.
4. Experiential markers *guo4* in Mandarin (Huang, 2003) and *gwo3* in Cantonese (Wong et al., 2003) indicate that the event has taken place prior to the time of speaking, with an emphasis on the experience.
5. The habitual marker *hoi1* in Cantonese is habitual and is comparable with the habitual expression in English (Stokes & Fletcher, 2003; Wong et al., 2003; Matthews & Yip, 2011).
6. The delimitative marker *haa2* (do… for a while) in Cantonese is regarded as a delimitative aspect form denoting the short duration of related actions (Wong et al., 2003). There are no habitual or delimitative aspects in Mandarin (Li & Shirai, 2000).

There is no consensus over the total number of aspect markers in Cantonese. For example, Cheung (1972) lists 7 types, Kwok (1971) suggests 11 and Fletcher and his colleagues (Fletcher et al., 2005; Stokes & Fletcher, 2000, 2003; Wong et al., 2003) list 6 as the benchmark in their comparisons of young children with normal and delayed language development.

The temporal adverb is another important temporal device in Chinese languages (Huang, 2006). Temporal adverbs in Mandarin can generally be classified into three sub-types: past time, present time and future time (Li & Shirai, 2000). But some adverbs can be used to express the frequency and duration of actions, either between the verb and the object, or after the verb and object, or with repetition of the transitive verb (Huang, 2003). We propose that these adverbs be classified into separate sub-types of temporal adverbs: the adverbs of frequency and duration. There might also be another sub-type of adverb that indicates the time sequencing of verbs, for example *sau2sin1* (at first), *jin4zi1hau6* (next), *zeoi3hau6* (at last). These may be labeled as adverbs of sequencing. In effect, it is argued that six subtypes of adverbs may be involved in temporal expression in Cantonese: past, present, future, frequency, duration and sequence. The study reported here sets out to test whether all the six subtypes of temporal adverbs can be detected in Cantonese-speaking preschoolers' natural utterances.

Last but not least, time expressions in Chinese languages include a set of nouns indicating the year, month, season, date, session, hour and minute of the occurrence of actions (Huang, 2006; Matthews & Yip, 2011). Dates and times are expressed in reverse order to that of English, going from large units to small units, beginning with the year and ending with the second. Thus the general formula is *XXXX nin4* (year) *XX jyut6* (month) *XX yat6* (day) *XX dim2* (o'clock) *XX fan1* (minute) *XX miu* (second). Since we could find no studies on whether Cantonese-speaking children are able to acquire this complicated system of temporality in their early years, we set out to investigate this issue in the current study.

1.2 Acquisition of Chinese temporality in the early years

Most studies of the acquisition of Chinese temporality feature Mandarin-speaking children and usually have two foci: the emergence and development of linguistic forms of temporality (aspect markers, temporal adverbs and nouns), and the relationship between aspect marking and the inherent lexical aspect (Huang, 2006). It has been reported that, generally, the perfective marker *le* emerges before the imperfective markers *zai* (progressive) and *zhe* (durative), which in turn appear before the experiential marker *guo* (Erbaugh, 1978, 1985, 1992; Lin, 1986). As for the relationship between aspect marking and the inherent lexical aspect, a strong association has been found to exist between the perfective aspect and telic verbs and between the imperfective aspect and atelic verbs (Erbaugh, 1992; Li, 1990; Li & Bowerman, 1998; Li & Shirai, 2000). These findings are consistent with the process-result distinction proposed by the basic child grammar hypothesis (Slobin, 1985).

It has been reported in the research on Mandarin temporal nouns and adverbs that 4- to 5-year-olds can comprehend nouns of today, yesterday and tomorrow; 5- to 6-year-olds can understand words denoting parts of the day, such as morning and afternoon; and 6-year-olds can comprehend words denoting longer periods of time such as "this year" or shorter time units such as "eight o' clock in the morning" (Zhu, Wu, Ying, Zhu, & Zhuang, 1982). It has been found that 4-year-olds have great difficulty making use of temporal devices to maintain story lines, whereas 6-year-olds demonstrate an ability to use more temporal and causal connectives (Chang, 1998). In summary, existing studies (Chang, 1998; Erbaugh, 1978, 1985, 1992; Huang, 2003; Li & Bowerman, 1998; Lin, 1986; Zhu et al, 1982) indicate that the acquisition of Mandarin temporality shares many similarities with that of children speaking other languages.

Studies of early temporality in Cantonese have, by and large, focused on early linguistic development, especially the acquisition of aspect forms in SLI children. Leung (1995) and Lee, Wong & Wong (1996) found that children were able to use the perfective marker *zo2* at 18 months, and later the imperfective *zyu6* at 24 months and *gan2* at 39 months. Mak (1993) found that both *zo2* and *gan2* could be used by children less than 30 months old. Nevertheless, it is widely believed that the emergence of grammatical morphemes with temporal meanings occurs around 3 years of age in Cantonese-speaking children, similar to young children speaking other languages (Fletcher et al., 2005; Lee, Wong, & Wong, 1996).

Comparisons of normal and SLI children indicate that *zo2* is used with similar frequency by both children with SLI and normally developing children (Stokes & Fletcher, 2000). However, 5-year-old normally developing children are able to produce aspect across different verb types whereas the SLI group restricts aspect to those verbs that can partner the semantics of the aspect marker with matched inherent temporal meaning (Stokes & Fletcher, 2003). For example, Wong et al. (2003) found that 5-year-olds with SLI tended to restrict the use of *zo2* to telic verbs, whereas normal children could extend its use to atelic verbs. All these findings imply that the use of aspect markers might be of value as a clinical marker of specific language impairment in Cantonese-speaking children.

The above review has elicited as many questions as answers. Most of the studies included in the review are based on data from relatively small numbers of children in artificially contrived situations. It can be argued whether such studies are able to yield with any authority the full range of the productive repertoire of temporal devices, in particular, the number of aspect markers produced by normally developing young children communicating spontaneously in naturalistic settings. Representative naturalistic data are urgently needed to establish developmental norms of temporal expression. Without these norms, studies of children with SLI lack a reliable benchmark. In an attempt to resolve these issues and to shed light on the early acquisition of Cantonese temporalities, the present study adopts a specifically designed free play task to elicit a large representative sample of young children's language in order to establish:

1. the number and types of temporal forms that can be identified in the productive repertoire of Cantonese-speaking young children;

2. whether there are age-related differences in the acquisition of temporal forms, in particular, the types and repertoire size.
3. whether Cantonese-speaking young children are able to acquire all the aspectual forms and, if so, the cognitive and educational implications of this knowledge.

2. Method

2.1 The Corpus

The Early Child Cantonese Corpus (ECCC) we established in the past decade (Tse et al., 2002; Tse, Chan, & Li, 2005; Tse, Li, & Leung, 2007) was used in this study. A language corpus can provide data for both qualitative and statistical analysis and may be further analyzed by third parties for multiple purposes. Its major limitation, however, is that the data can only represent a sample of the language under investigation, which might be potentially skewed in its content and pertinence for the wider scenario (Tse & Li, 2011). To minimize this potential problem, a corpus needs to be comprehensive and inclusive, and should be derived from a large sample with data collected from typical everyday contexts. ECCC is the largest corpus of Cantonese which contains speech samples of 492 children aged 36, 48 and 60 months collected in 30-minute free play sessions. The children were randomly sampled from each class in the 68 participating preschools (58 kindergartens and 10 nurseries) located in Hong Kong Island, Kowloon and the New Territories. There were 82 boys and 82 girls in each age group. The final database consisted of a total of 90,908 words from the 492 children, with a mean of 48.65 ($SD = 17.35$) utterances and a mean of 184.77 ($SD = 52.38$) words per child. The mean lengths of utterances (MLU) for 3-, 4-, and 5-year old groups were 5.72 ($SD = 1.04$), 5.96 ($SD = 1.11$) and 6.33 ($SD = 1.36$) respectively.

2.2 Communication task

ECCC collected spontaneous speech by the children in the same role-play activities, using identical sets of toys including cooking materials, food and fruit, furniture and electrical appliances, hospital materials and vehicles. Each randomly arranged pair of age-matched participants (boy/girl, boy/boy, or girl/girl) was left in the play corner to role play for 30 minutes. The children were encouraged to collaborate and communicate while they were playing with the toys, and the 30-minute long conversation that emerged was audio-recorded using an unobtrusive recorder. The task created a highly interactive and dynamic context that served as a natural outlet for the children to make spontaneous use of temporal words. During the play sessions, researchers observed but did not intervene and there were no other children present.

2.3 Coding of the linguistic forms and functions

The coding system that we have developed and validated in previous studies on early childhood Cantonese (Tse et al., 2002; Tse, Chan, & Li, 2005; Tse, Li, & Leung, 2007) was used in this study. The Cantonese coding system includes the typologies of different lexical forms (nouns, verbs, classifiers, temporal words, aspect markers, adverbs, etc.) and those of different pragmatic functions (interrogatives, locative and temporal functions, etc.). A panel of psycholinguists was engaged in finalizing the coding system for the linguistic forms of time and aspect. One of the researchers designed the computer program to automatically identify all the utterances involving these temporal words. The two researchers then analyzed and recoded the elicited utterances and words into different linguistic forms and functions. The inter-rater reliability was 93%. The panel of psycholinguists also scrutinized the coding results to achieve consensus on all the uncertain or unsolved coding items. All those non-temporal items were excluded from the statistics upon the approval of this panel.

It is important to note that the language samples as a whole were of varying length; thus absolute counts were not used directly in the analyses. In counting the number of temporal words produced by each child (See Table 1 and Table 2), for example, we only counted whether the child had used the word or not, not the number of times it had been used. In this way, we were able to count how many types of temporal word the children used, then the repertoire size of each age group. In other words, calculations are independent of utterance length.

3. Results

3.1 The developmental repertoires of temporal lexicons

Altogether three types of temporal words were identified from the utterances produced by the 492 participants: 62 nouns, 69 adverbs and 9 aspects. All the temporal words produced by the three age groups were analyzed and placed within the typology to permit identification of developmental trends. The results in Table 1 indicate that:

1. The first set of nouns produced by the 3-year-old Cantonese-speakers covered all the subtypes in the proposed typology, except for those of week and season. The season words *dung1gwai2/ dung1tin1* (winter) emerged in the 4-year-olds' utterances, whereas week words such as *seng1keiluk6* (Saturday)/ *seng1kei-4jat6* (Sunday) were only found in the 5-year-olds' expressions.

2. Altogether 32.3% of the new noun words were present in the 3-year-olds' utterances, 33.8% new nouns in those of the 4-year-olds and 33.8% new nouns in those of the 5-year-olds, representing an evenly increasing usage of new temporal nouns.

3. The adverbs produced by the 3-year-olds covered all the subtypes of future, past, sequence, frequency plus duration, and present expression, and 32.3% of these were present in the 3-year-olds' utterances, an additional 27.9 % in those of the 4-year-olds and further 16.2% in those of the 5-year-olds, representing a steady increase of new temporal adverbs.

4. All 9 aspects the cohort could have produced were found in the utterances produced by the three age groups, implying that there is no increase in the number of aspect types during this stage of childhood. It is important to note that once a term appeared at an earlier age it continued to be present in the speech of children of the older groups. Therefore items identified in a younger group are not listed for older groups in Table 1.

Table 1. List of the temporal devices produced by the Cantonese-speaking preschoolers (N = 492)

Temporal device	*Age 3:0 (n = 164)*	*Age 4: 0 (n = 164)*	*Age 5:0 (n = 164)*
Nouns of time (62*)			
Day (5)	*gam1jat6, ting1jat6, kam4jat6, dai6jat6*	*dang2jat6*	
Session (14)	*gam1maan5, kam-4maan5, je6maan5, gam1ziu1, tin1gwong1*	*je6maan5hak1, tin-1hak1, ting1ziu1zou2, jat1zou2, ziu1tau4zou2*	*ting1maan5, jat1ziu-1zou2, seng4maan5, aan3zau3*
Times (5)	*gam1ci3, haa6ci3, soeng6jat1ci3*	*soeng6ci3*	*gam1*
Week (3)			*seng1kei4luk6, seng-1kei4jat6, seng1kei4*
Season (4)		*dung1gwai3, dung1tin1*	*haa6tin1, gam1nin4,*
Hour (18)	*cat1dim2, luk6dim2, luk6dim2, sap6ji-6dim2, sap6jat1dim-2zung1*	*saam1dim2, ng5dim2, sap6dim2, sap6jat1dim2, gau2dim2, sei3dim-2zung1, jat1dim2, sap6ji-6dim2*	*gau2dim2zung1, ji6sap6dim2, baat3dim2, luk6dim-2zung1, saam1dim-2zung1*

Table 1. *(continued)*

Temporal device	*Age 3:0 (n = 164)*	*Age 4: 0 (n = 164)*	*Age 5:0 (n = 164)*
Minutes (13)	*luk6dim2daap6baat3, daap3bun3, gau2dim-2daap6gau2*	*fan1zung1, sap6fan-1zung1, gau2dim-2saam1, gau2dim2luk6, luk6dim2bun3*	*jat1dim2bun3, gau-2dim2ling4ng5fan1, baat3dim2gei2, sap6ji6dim2bun3, daap6zeng3sei3dim2*
Adverbs of time (69)			
Present (5)	*ji4gaa1, ji1gaa1, ne1zan6*	*ngaam4ngaam4, gne1aa1*	
Past (16)	*tau4sin1, zing6waa6, cau4sin1, ji5cin4, ji5ging1, kau4sin1, gau6si4, cung4cin4, zan6si4, go2si4, go2zan6*	*jau5jat1jat6, gwo2si4, zi1cin4, yun4loi4,*	*go2go3si4hau6*
Future (24)	*zau6lai4, jat1zan6, dai6jat6, ji5, dai6si4, zau6faai3, zik1hak1, dang2jat1zan6sin1, jat1zan6gaan1, dang2zan6, zau6, zan6gaan1sin1*	*zan6jat1gaan1sin1, dan-g2zan6gaan1sin1, zan-6gaan1, dang2zan6sin1, ji5hau6, jat1zan6sin1*	*cung4gam1ji5hau6, ji5haa6lok6nei4, go2si4zan6, dan-g2jat1zan6gaan1, dai6ji6si4, dang2jat-1zan6*
Frequency + duration (11)	*jat1zan6, si4si4, jau-5si4zan6, seng4jat6, jau5si4, jat1zan6sin1, jat1zan6gaan1*	*zan6, ceoi4si4*	*jau5paai4, zan6gaan-1sin1*
Sequence (13)	*sin1, sin1zi3, hau-6mei5, hau6, sau2sin1*	*zi1hau6jin4, ji5hau6, sau1mei5, zeoi3hau6, zi1hau6, zeot1zi1*	*zung1yu1, maan5*
Aspects of time (9)	*zo2, jyun4, zyu6, gan2, gwo3, zoek6, saai3, liu5, haa2*		
Repertoire size	*67*	*109*	*140*

Note. *.The value in brackets represents the subtotal of corresponding subtype words produced by the sample (N = 492).

The number and relative percentage of each subtype within the subcategories were calculated and are shown in Table 1. The results indicate that almost half (49.31%) of the temporal words were adverbs, many of which (43.75%) were nouns, and few (6.94%) were aspectual forms. Within noun words, hour and minute expressions accounted for 21.53%, session words for 9.72%, day and time words both for 3.47%, season for 2.78% and week for 2.08%. Within the subcategory of adverb, the subtypes of future, past, sequence, frequency plus duration and present accounted for 16.67%, 11.11%, 9.03%, 8.33%, 4.17%, respectively, indicating that future adverb is the most common subtype with most variants and that present adverb is the least common. It is interesting to observe that the adverbial phrase *dang2*(A) *jat1*(B) *zan6*(C) *gaan1*(D) *sin1*(E) was frequently used to express future time by the children in a set of colloquial variations such as AC, ABC, ACE, ABCD, ABCE, ABDE, BC, BCE, BCE, BCDE, CD, CDE (see Table 1). This observation might explain why future adverbs accounted for a relatively higher percentage in the repertoire. In Mandarin Chinese, there are not so many variations in this type of time expression.

3.2 The developmental changes in time expression

Chi-Square analyses were conducted on contingency tables for repertoire size, nouns, and adverbs produced by 3-, 4- and 5-year-olds, taking care to avoid any instance of statistical dependence among contingencies. As shown in Figure 1, the results indicate significant differences between the three age groups in the distributions of repertoire size [χ^2 (2, $N=492)=25.49$, $p<.001$], nouns [χ^2 (2, $N=492)=21.36$, $p<.001$] and adverbs [χ^2 (2, $N=492)=8.99$, $p<.05$]. A contingency table was drawn up and tested statistically for the strength of differences, if any, in the top 10 temporal terms with the highest distribution frequency among the 492 sample. As shown in Table 2, no significant age differences were found in these commonly used temporal terms, except for *sin1* (adverb) and *jyun4* (aspect). This seems to indicate that 8 of the top 10 temporal terms had been acquired by age 3. It is important to note that 5 of the top 10 temporal words are aspectual forms, 4 are adverbs and 1 a noun *gam1jat6* (today).

Frequencies of occurrence (including repeated usage) of 9 aspect markers were calculated for each child, and the means and standard deviations are presented in Table 3. It was found that *zo2, saai3, haa2, jyun4* and *zyu6* were frequently used by the children, and their means of frequency of occurrence were around 1 or more. In addition, all these aspect markers were widely used with different types of verbs, including telic and atelic verbs and punctual and unpunctual verbs. Among the aspect markers, *zo2* was the most frequently ($M>2.6$) and widely used to the extent that it could occur with 161 verbs. A MANOVA analysis was conducted to test for possible differences in the frequencies with Age (3) X Gender (2) as between-subject variables. The analysis indicates no significant main effects for Age, Gender or interaction of Age X Gender in the productivity of 9 aspect markers, except for *hou2*, $F(1, 3)=3.37$, $p<.05$. This finding suggests that aspect markers might not be a very sensitive indicator of language development between 3 to 5 years old, whereas *hou2* might be so.

Table 2. Age differences in top 10 temporal devices with the highest distributed frequency in the sample (N = 492)

	Temporal word	Type	Age 3	Age 4	Age 5	χ^2	Utterance
1	o左 *zo2*	Aspect	100	105	116	3.6	WONG: *ngo5 cit3 zo2 keoi5 sin1.* English: I chop it first.
2	先 *sin1*	Adverb	89	103	113	7.5*	WONG: *ngo5 cit3 je5 sik6 sin1 laa1.* English: I chop something to eat first.
3	完 *jyun4*	Aspect	39	48	65	10.0**	WONG: *ngo5 soeng2 tai2 jyun4 ne1 bun2 jau6 jat1 bun2.* English: I want to read one after another.
4	而家 *ji4gaa1*	Adverb	42	54	46	2.2	WONG: *ji4gaa1 ne1dou6 dou1 jung4 saai3 gaa3l aa1.* English: Now it has already melted away.
5	住 *zyu6*	Aspect	36	53	47	4.5	WONG: *tai2 zyu6…* English: look at (it)
6	緊 *gan2*	Aspect	26	20	30	2.4	WONG: *ji1gaa1 ngo5 doek3 gan2 nei5go3 BB.* English: Now I am kissing your baby.
7	過 *gwo3*	Aspect	28	20	23	1.6	WONG: *nei5 aa1 jaa6 gei2 nin4 cin4 dou1 faat3 gwo3 siu1.* English: You have had fever twenty years ago.
8	今日 *gam1jat6*	Noun	12	16	12	0.9	WONG: *ngo5 gam1jat6 ng4 zyu2 faan6.* English: I won't cook today.
9	就o黎 *zau6nei4*	Adverb	13	10	13	0.5	WONG: *zau6 lai4 dak1 laa3.* English: Almost finished.
10	一陣間 *jat1zan6gaan1*	Adverb	8	6	13	3.1	WONG: *jat1zan6gaan1mok1zo2.* English: shell it in a while.

Note. *p* < .05. ** *p* < .01. *** *p* < .001.

Table 3. Age differences in frequencies of aspect markers produced by the Cantonese-speaking preschoolers (N = 492)

| Chinese | WONG | Meaning | Age 3; 0 | | Age 4; 0 | | Age 5;0 | | F value | Types of verb involved |
			M	SD	M	SD	M	SD		
咗	*zo2*	Perfective	3.12	4.58	2.85	2.61	2.61	2.35	.19	161
完	*jyun4*	Perfective	.78	1.24	1.03	1.91	1.27	1.7	.86	35
住	*zyu6*	Continuous	.95	1.45	1.33	2.12	.90	1.27	.35	61
緊	*gan2*	Progressive	.45	.94	.68	2.1	.56	1.01	.46	38
過	*gwo3*	Experiential	.69	1.43	.58	1.45	.61	1.12	.12	29
著	*zoek6*	Perfective	0	0	.06	.23	.05	.22	.08	4
吓	*haa2*	Delimitative	1.17	2.05	1.69	1.85	1.52	1.95	.24	58
晒	*saai3*	Perfective	1.17	1.66	1.73	2.82	1.59	2.22	1.43	74
好	*hou2*	Perfective	.41	.84	.71	1.31	1.12	1.75	3.98*	28

Note. *$p < .05$.

3.3 Double aspectual marking and inappropriate use of temporal devices

Several instances of double aspectual marking were found in the data. Altogether 6 types of two-aspect compounds were identified from the utterances: *hou2-saai3* was widely used with 8 types of verbs, and the others such as *gwo3-saai3, hou2-zo2, zyu6-zo2, zoek6-zo2, jyun4-saai3* were used with one specified verb. For example, *zap1* **hou2-saai3** means *(have) tidied up* **completely** *and* **holistically**, *sik6 gwo3-saai3* indicates **all** *(the food) has* **already** *been eaten, baai2* **hou2-zo2** *implies (have) put into place* **appropriately** *and* **completely**, *gam6* **zyu6-zo2** *means have* **already** *been pressing, fan3* **zoek6-zo2** *indicates (have)* **already fallen** *asleep, and jam2* **jyun4-saai3** *means (have)* **completely** *drunk* **up**.

Three instances of misplacing aspects were found in the corpus, and one case of misusing temporal nouns was found in the study. The four cases are presented and analyzed as follows:

1. Example of misplacing *zo2*, three-year-old boy:
   Utterance: *ngo5 zek3 sau2 sau6 soeng1 **zo2** aa1 !*
   Corrected: *ngo5 zek3 sau2 sau6 **zo2** soeng1 aa1 !*
   English: My [CL] hand got wound [ASP] [SPF]?

2. Example of misplacing *zo2*, four-year-old girl:
   Utterance: *ngo5 dei6 bun1 **zo2** hei2 zoeng1 toi2 laa1 !*
   Corrected: *ngo5 dei6 bun1 hei2 **zo2** zoeng1 toi2 laa1 !*
   English: We [GEN] lift up [ASP] table [SPF]

3. Example of misplacing *saai3*, five-year-old girl:
    Utterance: *nei4 di1 saam1 keoi5 gaa3, jau6 faat3 mou4 **saai3**.*
    Corrected: *nei4 di1 saam1 keoi5 gaa3, jau6 faat3 **saai3** mou4.*
    English: This [GEN] clothes his [SPF], also go moldy [ASP].

These "misplacing" cases suggest that children in the sample of three different groups had acquired the notion that semantically an aspect marker is needed in an utterance to describe the situation. Syntactically, however, the children misplace it, confusing it with the associated verbs.

4. Example of semantically misplaced temporal nouns, four-year-old girl:
    Utterance: *nei5 aa1 jaa6 gei2 nin4 cin4 dou1 faat3 **gwo3** siu1.*
    English: You [SPF] twenty several years ago also had [ASP] fever.
    Translation: You have had a fever twenty years ago.

The girl in the above excerpt used *gwo3* to refer to an experiential action that took place prior to the time of speaking, almost "twenty years ago". But her listener was a 4-year-old preschooler, and this is a case of semantically misplaced temporal nouns associated with the concept of year. The girl might not have realized that her role play partner would not have been able to have a fever "twenty years ago".

The evidence that there was no change in the repertoire size ($N=9$) of aspectual markers (see Table 2 and Figure 1) and no age-related differences in frequency

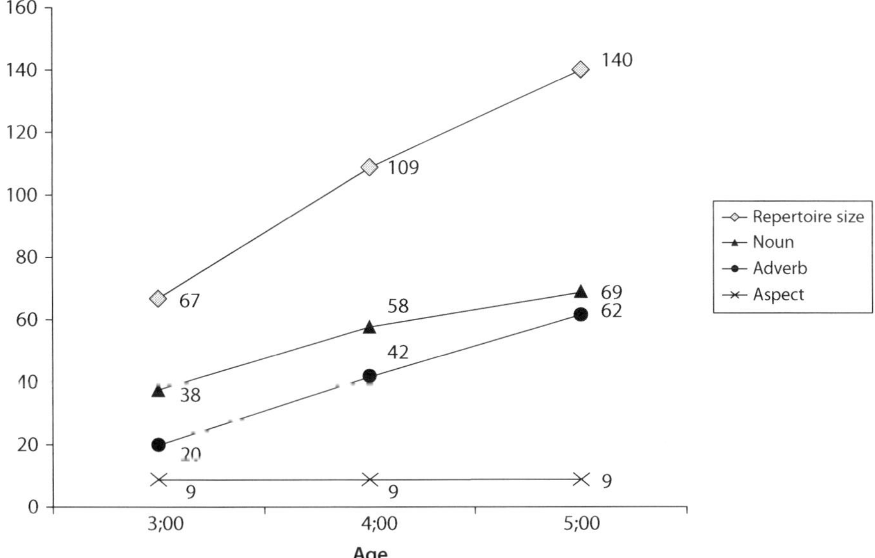

Figure 1. Mean number of temporal words and repertoire size produced by three age groups ($N = 492$)

of occurrence between 3 and 6 years old seems to suggest that, by 3-years of age, Cantonese-speaking children actually understand that an aspectual marker is needed when articulating the status of an action, and that the 9 aspect markers have already and completely emerged.

4. Discussion

4.1 Acquisition of temporal devices by Cantonese speakers in the early years

This study found remarkable changes in the repertoires of temporal lexicon in the Cantonese-speaking children with the types of nouns and adverbs increasing with age. It is important to note that the first set of temporal nouns uttered by the 3-year-olds did not cover all the subtypes listed in Table 1. The nouns of week and seasons, representing relatively larger-scale time concepts, were not found in the 3-year-olds' expressions. Several 4-year-olds had started using *dung1gwai3* and *dung1tin1* to talk about *winter*, while several 5-year-olds could use *seng1kei4luk6* (Saturday), *seng1kei4jat6* (Sunday) and *seng1kei4* (week) to talk about the *week-end*. This indicates that Cantonese-speaking children are likely to acquire the concepts of season and week until 5 years of age. The case of misused temporal nouns about years found in the transcripts seems to indicate that some 4-year-olds did not really understand "year" nouns, although they were able to use them syntactically. This possibility needs to be examined empirically in further studies to rule out the effects of sampling and the form of the communicative task used in the present study.

Regarding the acquisition of temporal adverbs, it is important to note that the set of temporal adverbs uttered by the 3-year-olds covered all the subtypes listed in Table 1. This indicates that the semantic differentiation of time expression set by the 6 subtypes has already emerged in the 3-year-olds' speech and that the children have acquired the temporal forms associated with the concepts of past, present, future, frequency, duration and sequence. Furthermore, it is interesting to see that the subtype of future adverbs co-occurs with most variants, whereas that of present adverbs is the least frequent. However, the naturalistic method used in the study limits the chances for obtaining sufficient evidence for this issue. It would be speculative to attribute the differences between the use of future and present adverbs to Cantonese linguistic features, preschooler's developmental features, the nature of the communicative task, or the combinations of all three. Nevertheless, although altogether 12 colloquial variations of the adverbial phrase *dang2* (A) *jat1* (B) *zan6* (C) *gaan1* (D) *sin1* (E) were found in the utterances of the children, most of these alternatives are not listed in Cantonese grammar books and therefore not explicitly taught at school. However, they are frequently used in daily conversations among adults so Cantonese-speaking preschoolers might have acquired variations by listening to adult conversation.

In total, 9 aspect markers were found in the utterances produced by the 3-, 4-, and 5-year-olds and there were no significant developmental differences in usage, except for *hou2*. Given the normative nature of the data reported by this chapter, we propose that the number of aspects in the repertoire of early child Cantonese should be set at 9, more than the baseline 6 widely used in many published psycholinguistic studies (Fletcher et al., 2005; Stokes & Fletcher, 2000, 2003; Wong et al., 2003), and that, by 3-years of age, normal children might have acquired these aspects. The additional three aspect markers, *hou2, jyun4, saai3*, were also frequently used by the children in the study. Thus, it might be possible that some widely used lists underestimate the proficiency of normal Cantonese-speaking children in terms of using aspect markers. Another area for exploration that arises from the data is that the study found significant differences in the frequency of producing *hou2* among the three age groups. This implies that *hou2* might possibly be used as a developmental indicator of language acquisition and even a clinical marker of delayed language development. A larger scale study is needed specifically to establish a definitive baseline for aspectual acquisition by Cantonese speaking children.

4.2 Acquisition of time concepts in the early years

A major objective of the study was to map age differences in the acquisition of tense and temporality by young children and to gain insight into cognitive underpinnings. There were statistically significant age differences in terms of the size of repertoire for nouns and adverbs, reflecting an age-related gain in the acquisition of the concept of time. Friedman (2000, 2003) proposes that children's difficulty in acquiring time concepts is due to the nature of their mental representations of events and the language habitually used to refer to time. The language that children from 2- to 7-years of age use to talk about past and future events reflects the emergence of the time concept. This confirms that the repertoire of temporal nouns and adverbs produced by the Cantonese-speaking preschoolers in the study increases with their age. In Piagetian terminology (Piaget, 1951), children must possess the ability to reflect "operatively" on the concept of time before they can securely grasp and use appropriate words and language to "dress" their thoughts.

Consistent with Friedman's studies (1977, 1986, 1992, 2000), the present study found that "season" and "week" words were not produced by children younger than 4 and 5 years old. Friedman found that until 7 to 8-years of age, children could not accurately talk about time events in terms of the days of weeks, and that estimation of timeline intervals or distances is not equivalent to that of adults until children are at least 10 years of age. An understanding of how conventional time terminology maps onto clock and calendar time only begins to appear between the age of 8 and 10 (Friedman, 2000). The present study also found that the only noun in the top 10 temporal words was *gam1jat6* (today). This finding is in line with studies in an experimental context (Friedman, 2003) in which 4-year-olds display some element of understanding of terms such as yesterday and today. This enables them to display a surface level of understanding that allows them to make explicit distinctions and judgments of yesterday and today. However, the conceptual understanding underlying this performance is insecure and inconsistent and derives from hearing snatches of conversations in which speakers talk about events happening tomorrow, today, and yesterday (Friedman, 2003). Although the present study found cross-linguistic evidence from Cantonese to support Friedman's finding, the reader should note that the preschoolers' time concept was quite limited: although they had good ideas of concepts such as *day, hour* and *minute*, they were still in the process of acquiring more advanced temporal concepts such as *week, season* and *year*.

Nevertheless, it is understandable that time, as a concept, does not appear in the concrete world of the child as "a physical entity to be discovered through exploration and manipulation" (Hudson, 2006, p. 71). It is socially construed and described through language exchanges; hence talking about past and future events is critical for the development of a differentiated concept of time (Nelson, 1996). This is verified by the cross-linguistic evidence in the present study. For example, in the utterance "*nei5 aa1 jaa6 gei2 nin4 cin4 dou1 faat3 gwo3 siu1*" (you have had a fever twenty years ago), both parties in the conversation were less than 5 years of age. This utterance sounds like an attempt to imitate a sentence spoken by the mother of the child in question to her father at home, and does not mean that the child had securely acquired the concept of years. Such temporal references to daily events provide input that helps with children's development of concepts of time (Friedman, 2000; Nelson, 1996). Children do not need to have a mature understanding of temporal terms (as in this case) in order to benefit from exposure to temporal language in conversations (Hudson, 2006). They may actually benefit from this kind of exposure because "hearing temporal language used in the context of thinking about everyday events promotes further conceptual development" (Hudson, 2006, p. 92). Furthermore, according to Vygotsky (1962), speech is a very powerful psychological tool that lays the foundation for basic structures of thinking later in one's development. In this case, the new word *nin4* (year) might be *interpsychological,* that is, learned through interaction with others on the social level. Later, this knowledge will become *intrapsychological,* being internally mastered on an individual level.

4.3 Acquisition of the pragmatics of time expression in the early years

The study revealed that, by 3-years of age, the Cantonese-speaking children examined had acquired semantic and syntactical aspects and used aspect *zo2* widely and frequently in peer communications. This finding accords with previous studies (see Fletcher et al., 2005; Lee et al., 1996; Leung, 1995) which suggest that the perfective marker *zo2* is the first aspect marker acquired by 21-month-olds. There are no obligatory contexts for aspect morphemes and verbs without aspects are grammatically acceptable (Stokes & Fletcher, 2003; Wong et al., 2003). It is thus interesting to ask why Cantonese-speaking young children master *zo2* very early and use it frequently and widely in peer conversations. This phenomenon might be associated with the nature of the aspectual system of Cantonese and that of the communication task in the present study.

The insertion of aspect form in Cantonese speech is constrained by pragmatic factors associated with speakers' perceptions of the temporal issue of the event and with whether they want to limit the addressee's interpretation (Fletcher et al., 2005). Similarly, Smith (1997), talking about the pragmatic role of the optionality of aspect forms in Mandarin, says that omitting an aspect form "triggers the neutral viewpoint, which is flexible in interpretation" (p. 279). In contrast, insertion of an aspect marker may not only stress the specific temporal character of the incident but also limit the set of interpretations available to the addressee (Fletcher et al., 2005). Therefore, the wide use of *zo2* in the children's communicative speech might be related to the fact that they tended to stress the completed status of their actions to their partners when involved in the highly interactive play context. This implies that pragmatic affordances may have a notable impact on the use of aspectual morphemes in Cantonese.

In addition, it is widely believed that the perfective aspect *zo2* combines naturally with telic verbs which describe changes of state (achievement or accomplishment) that have ended by the time the utterance is produced (Wong et al., 2003). The present study, however, found that the perfective marker *zo2* largely and frequently occurred with both telic and atelic verbs such as *have meal, watch TV, jump* and so on. It seems that the children were able to use aspect markers in the peer conversations to stress their views on the situations, and have gone beyond telic verbs. Whether or not being able to extend its use to atelic verbs is the very difference between the 5-year-olds with SLI and 3-year-old normal children in Wong et al. (2003). The present study verified this finding with representative normal children and indicates that some aspect markers (e.g., *hou2*) and their use could be used as clinical markers of specific language impairment in Cantonese-speaking young children.

The study also found instances of double aspectual marking in the utterances, such as *gwo3-saai3, hou2-zo2, zyu6-zo2, zoek6-zo2, jyun4-saai3*. Case analyses indicate that all these double aspect markers were used to strengthen two dimensions of the results associated with predicate verbs: the wholeness and accomplishment of actions. This implies that the Cantonese-speaking preschoolers studied deliberately emphasized the completed status and were concerned about the result status. This finding lends further support to the process-result distinction proposed by the basic child grammar hypothesis (Slobin, 1985), rather than the state-process distinction in Bickerton's (1984) language bio-program hypothesis. This phenomenon might also be associated with the two functions that Cantonese aspect markers serve in daily communication: the first aspect marker in these cases might be the "situation aspect" (Smith, 1983) or "lexical aspect" (Li & Bowerman, 1998), which refers to the temporal meaning inherent in the lexical items describing the situation. The second marker might be the "viewpoint aspect" (Smith, 1983, 1997) or "grammatical aspect" (Li & Bowerman, 1998), which emphasize the speaker's viewpoint of the temporal contours of the event described in an utterance as recently completed. Clearly, this double aspectual marking behaviour merits further study.

5.   Conclusion

In conclusion, a productive repertoire of temporal devices used by Cantonese-speaking young children has been proposed; a typology of Cantonese temporality has been established; and the aspectual system of young Cantonese-speakers has been confirmed. No differences were found in the development and usage of aspect markers, but some instances of double aspectual marking and misplacing aspects were found. This study has also uncovered some developmental trends worth exploring further.

This study has potential to contribute to the literature in two ways: First, it studied a large representative sample of Cantonese-speaking young children, N = 492. This sample size has not been achieved in previous studies (For review, see Tse and Li, 2011). Second, this study gathered authentic data from exchanges in a naturalistic "child-play" context, whereas other Cantonese studies elicited data with experimental approaches. However, the study has its limitations. First, it targeted a cross-sectional rather than a longitudinal sample and, second, the age range examined should, in hindsight, have been extended in order to compare with other published research.

As it stands, the study offers a descriptive account of children's development of time expressions. Although its design and scope do not permit the researchers to comment precisely on how the children's language has longitudinally developed, the typology and repertoire found in the study provide a model for further research, theory building and language learning. Cantonese language educators might amend and design grammar books in light of the authentic speech production of the young children; and language teachers might find the study helpful in understanding ways to facilitate the development of tense and aspect in young children. The finding that young Cantonese-speaking children might not be able to name weekdays properly before 5 years of age should be noted by early childhood educators. Young children should be given opportunities in which they can practise using the terms correctly and repeatedly. The considerable variability of the children's language also suggests a need for further study of Cantonese temporality.

Note: *Cantonese examples are given in the Romanization scheme developed by Wong Shik Ling (also known as S. L. Wong), in which tones are numbered from 1 (high level) to 6 (low level). The online edition of S. L. Wong's Chinese Syllabary is available at http://humanum.arts.cuhk.edu.hk/Lexis/Canton/.*

Acknowledgments

This work was partially supported by the GRF Fund (RGC Ref No. 747109), HKSAR. Thanks go to Dr. Sylvia Opper for her invaluable input in developing the project. We also like to thank Dr. Terry Dolan, Ms. S. K. Leung, Ms. W. Y. Chio, Dr. C. Chan, Ms. S. M. Kwong, Mr. W. J. Lau, Ms. L. Y. Fung, Miss Eileen Wong, Miss Jessie Wong and the children and staff at participating preschools. Correspondence concerning this article should be addressed to Dr. Hui Li at the Faculty of Education, The University of Hong Kong, Hong Kong. Electronic mail may be sent to huili@ hku.hk.

References

Aksu-Koc, Ayhan. 1998. "The Role of Input vs. Universal Predispositions in the Emergence of Tense-aspect Morphology: Evidence from Turkish". *First Language* 18.255–280.
Antinucci, Francesco & Miller, Ruth. 1976. "How Children Talk about What Happened". *Journal of Child Language* 3.167–189.
Bickerton, Derek. 1984. "The Language Bioprogram Hypothesis". *The Behavioral and Brain Sciences* 7.173–221.
Cao, Defang, Wenjie Li, Chunfa Yuan & Wong, Kam-Fai. 2006. "Automatic Chinese Aspectual Classification Using Linguistic Indicators". *International Journal of Information Technology* 12:4.99–109.
Chang, Chien-Ju. 1998. "The Development of Autonomy in Preschool Mandarin Chinese-Speaking Children's Play Narratives". *Narrative Inquiry* 8:1.77–111.

Chao, Yuen Ren. 1968. *A grammar of spoken Chinese*. Berkeley, Calif.: University of California Press.

Chen, Jidong & Shirai, Yasuhiro. 2010. "The Development of Aspectual Marking in Child Mandarin Chinese". *Applied Psycholinguistics* 31:1.1–28.

Cheung, Hung Nin Samuel. 1972. *Study on Hong Kong Cantonese Grammar* (in Chinese). Hong Kong: The Chinese University of Hong Kong.

Erbaugh, Mary S. 1978. "Acquisition of Temporal and Aspectual Distinctions in Mandarin". *Papers and Reports on Child Language Development* 15.30–36.

Erbaugh, Mary S. 1985. "Personal Involvement and the Development of Language for Time-Aspect". *Papers and Reports on Child Language Development* 26.54–61.

Erbaugh, Mary S. 1992. "The Acquisition of Mandarin". *The Cross-Linguistic Study of Language Acquisition* ed. by Dan Isaac Slobin, vol. 3, 373–443. Hillsdale, New Jersey: Lawrence Erlbaum Associates.

Fletcher, Paul, Laurence B. Leonard, Stephanie F. Stokes & Anita M.-Y. Wong. 2005. "The Expression of Aspect in Cantonese-Speaking Children with Specific Language Impairment". *Journal of Speech, Language, and Hearing Research* 48:3.621–634.

Friedman, William J. 1977. "The Development of Children's Understanding of Cyclic Aspects of Time". *Child Development* 48.1593–1599.

Friedman, William J. 1986. "The Development of Children's Knowledge of Temporal Structure". *Child Development* 57.1386–1400.

Friedman, William J. 1992. "The Development of Children's Representations of Temporal Structure". *Time, action, and cognition: Towards bridging the gap* ed. by Francoise Macar, Viviane Pouthas & William J. Friedman, 67–75. Boston: Kluwer Academic.

Friedman, William J. 2000. "The Development of Children's Knowledge of the Times of Future Events". *Child Development* 71.913–932.

Friedman, William J. 2003. "The Development of a Differentiated Sense of the Past and the Future". *Advances in Child Development and Behavior* ed. by Robert Kail, vol. 31, 229–269. New York: Academic Press.

Huang, Chiung-Chih. 2003. "Mandarin Temporality Inference in Child, Maternal and Adult Speech". *First Language* 23:2.147–169.

Huang, Chiung-Chih. 2006. "Child Language Acquisition of Temporality in Mandarin Chinese". *The Handbook of East Asian psycholinguistics* ed. by Ping Li, Li Hai Tan, Elizabeth Bates & Ovid J.L. Tzeng, vol. I, 52–60. Cambridge, UK: Cambridge University Press.

Hudson, Judith A. 2006. "The Development of Future Time Concepts through Mother–Child Conversation". *Merrill-Palmer Quarterly* 52:1.70–95.

Kwok, Helen. 1971. *A Linguistic Study of the Cantonese Verb*. Hong Kong: Centre of Asian Studies, The University of Hong Kong.

Lee, Thomas H.T., Wong, C. H. & C. S.P. Wong. 1996. "Functional Categories in Child Cantonese". *The Development of Grammatical Competence in Cantonese-Speaking Children: Report of Hong Kong RGC* ed. by Thomas H.-T. Lee, C. H. Wong, C. S. Leung, P. Man, A. Cheung, K. Szeto & C. S.-P. Wong, Ear-marked Grant 1991–1994, 155–174. Hong Kong: RGC.

Leung, Cheung Shing. 1995. *The Development of Aspect Markers in a Cantonese-Speaking Child between the Ages of 21 and 45 Months*. Unpublished doctoral dissertation. University of Hawaii, Manoa.

Li, Ping. 1990. *Aspect and Aktionsart in Child Mandarin*. Unpublished doctoral dissertation, University of London.

Li, Ping & Bowerman, Melissa. 1998. "The Acquisition of Lexical and Grammatical Aspect in Chinese". *First Language* 18:3.311–350.

Li, Ping & Shirai, Yasuhiro. 2000. *The Acquisition of Lexical and Grammatical Aspect.* Berlin: Mouton de Gruyter.

Lin, Hwei-Jane. 1986. *A Developmental Study of Acquisition of Aspect Markers in Chinese Children.* Unpublished master's thesis. Fu Jen Catholic University, Taiwan.

Luk, Wing Shan. 2001. *The Production of Aspect Marker in Cantonese-Speaking Children: An Experimental Study.* Unpublished bachelor's dissertation, The University of Hong Kong, Hong Kong.

Mak, Lena Ah Yee. 1993. *Cantonese-Speaking Children's Use of the Aspect Markers "jo" and "gan" in Three Experimental Tasks.* Unpublished Master's dissertation, The University of Hong Kong, Hong Kong.

Matthews, Stephen & Yip, Virginia. 2011. *Cantonese: A Comprehensive Grammar* (2nd edition). London, UK: Routledge.

Nelson, Katherine. 1996. *Language in Cognitive Development: The Emergence of the Mediated Mind.* New York: Cambridge University Press.

Piaget, Jean. 1951. *Play, dreams and imagination.* New York, USA: Norton.

Shirai, Y., Slobin, D. I., & R. E, Weist. (1998). Introduction: The acquisition of tense-aspect morphology. *First Language* 18.254–253.

Slobin, Dan. 1985. "Cross-linguistic Evidence of the Language-Making Capacity". *The Cross-linguistic Study of Language Acquisition* ed. by Dan Isaac Slobin, vol. 2, 1157–1249. Hillsdale, New Jersey: Lawrence Erlbaum Associates.

Smith, Carlota S. 1983. "A Theory of Aspectual Choice". *Language* 59:3.479–501.

Smith, Carlota S. 1997. *The Parameter of Aspect* (2nd ed.). Dordrecht, Netherlands: Kluwer Academic.

Stokes, Stephanie F. & Fletcher, Paul. 2000. "Lexical Diversity and Productivity in Cantonese-Speaking Children with Specific Language Impairment". *International Journal of Language and Communication Disorders* 35.527–541.

Stokes, Stephanie F. & Fletcher, Paul. 2003. "Aspectual Forms in Cantonese Children with Specific Language Impairment". *Linguistics* 41.381–406.

Tse, Shek Kam, Carol Chan, Hui Li & Kwong, Sin Mee. 2002. "Sex Differences in Syntactic Development: Evidence from Cantonese-Speaking Preschoolers in Hong Kong". *International Journal of Behavioural Development* 26:6.509–517.

Tse, Shek Kam, Carol Chan, Hui Li & Sin Mee Kwong, Carol K.K. Chan & Li, Hui. 2005. "Is the Expressive Vocabulary of Young Cantonese Speaker Noun or Verb Dominated?" *Early Child Development and Care* 175:3.215–227.

Tse, Shek Kam, Carol Chan, Hui Li & Sin Mee Kwong, Carol K.K. Chan & Li, Hui. 2011. *Early Child Cantonese: Facts and Implications.* Berlin, Germany: Mouton de Gruyter.

Tse, Shek Kam, Carol Chan, Hui Li & Sin Mee Kwong, Carol K.K. Chan, Hui Li & On Leung, Shing. 2007. "The Acquisition of Cantonese Classifiers by Preschool Children in Hong Kong". *Journal of Child Language* 34:2.495–517.

Vygotsky, Lev Semenovich. 1962. *Thought and Language.* Cambridge, Mass.: MIT Press.

Weist, Richard M., Marja Atanassova, Hanna Wysocka & Pawlak, Aleksandra. 1999. "Spatial and Temporal Systems in Child Language and Thought: A Cross-linguistic Study". *First Language* 19.267–311.

Wong, Anita M.-Y, Stephanie F. Stokes & Fletcher, Paul. 2003. "Collocational Diversity in Perfective Aspect zo2 Use in Cantonese Children with SLI". *Journal of Multilingual Communication Disorders* 1:2.132–140.

Zhu, Man-shu. Jing-zhi Wu, H. Ying, L. Zhu, & Zhuang, Xiu-juan. 1982. "Children's Comprehension of Several Kinds of Temporal Words in Sentences". *Acta Psychologica Sinica* 3.294–301.

Maternal affective input in mother–child interaction

A cross-cultural perspective*

Zhuo Jing-Schmidt
University of Oregon

Contrastive analysis of Chinese and American maternal affective speech acts revealed significant differences in the quantity of child-directed positive and negative speech acts. There were also important qualitative differences in specific types of maternal affective input. Results are consistent with available knowledge of cross-cultural differences in parenting approaches, and have implications for cross-cultural emotional and pragmatic development. Differential cultural values were addressed to account for the observed linguistic behaviors.

1.   Introduction

Different cultures provide different contexts for understanding parental approaches and maternal communicative styles, which reflect cultural values and priorities. In a storm of national controversy in the USA unleashed by Amy Chua's memoir *Battle Hymn of the Tiger Mother* (2011) and her provocatively titled article in the *Wall Street Journal*, "Why Chinese Mothers Are Superior", the culture-specificity of parenting style and its developmental consequences were brought into the spotlight. In the media and for the general public, Chinese mothers suddenly became "tiger mothers" associated with a parenting style characterized by high expectation, strict control, ruthless coercion, disregard of individuality, and near military discipline. Yet cultural differences in parenting are no novelty to scholars of cross-cultural psychology, child development, and education. It is well established that Chinese

* This research was supported by the Center for Intercultural Dialogue, University of Oregon. Maram Epstein, Deborah Grant, Alice McLerran, Reba Simon, Tze-lan Sang, and Hongyin Tao offered insightful comments on an earlier draft, for which I am deeply grateful. I also thank the editors and reviewers for their valuable suggestions. As ever, I am responsible for all remaining errors in the writing.

parenting centers on the child's academic success as the ultimate goal, which motivates extensive and intensive parental investment and involvement in the child's schooling (Chao 1994, 1995, 1996, 2001; Chao & Tseng 2002; Stevenson et al. 1993). What is less noted is that it is language that constitutes and mediates cultural actions and activities including parenting practices, both explicitly and implicitly. It is language that affords to parents and caregivers semiotic resources for socializing children into the social order and cultural values of their community (Ochs & Schieffelin 2011). Given the cultural differences in the ideology, expression, and perception of emotion and in the semantics and pragmatics of emotion (Rosaldo 1980; Levy 1984; Markus & Kitayama 1991, 1994; Wierzbicka 1994, 1999; 2003), affective language in particular occupies a salient place in constituting parenting style and in transmitting cultural beliefs and values (Ochs 1986). However, with the exception of Lo and Fung's (2011) study of shaming as a corrective strategy in child-rearing practice in Taiwan, little is known of culture-specific uses of affective language by Chinese parents in interaction with their children. Much less is known of cross-cultural patterns in this domain, save studies of shaming, teasing and directives (Schieffelin 1986; Eisenberg 1986; Miller 1986; Clancy 1986; Lo & Fung 2011). It is the goal of this chapter to investigate the affective verbal input given by Chinese and American mothers to their children in spontaneous everyday interaction.

Research in first language acquisition provides robust evidence that maternal linguistic input impacts child language development and performance (Hampson & Nelson 1993; Murray et al. 1990; Tomasello & Todd 1983; Baker & Nelson 1984; Bates et al. 1988; Farrar 1990), while research in developmental psychology indicates that affective forms of input are salient in children's psychological development. Young children's recognition and response to maternal emotion signals (Cohn & Tronick 1983; Klinnert 1984; Sorce & Emde 1981) and the influence of maternal affect on child emotional development in infancy and early childhood (Belsky et al. 1984; Emde et al. 1978; Boccia & Campos 1989; Lagacé Séguin & Coplan 2005) are well documented. There is an intrinsic link between maternal interactive input and child emotional, behavioral, and physiological regulation (Bowlby 1969, 1976; Bloom 1993; Main et al. 1979; Calkins et al. 1998; Shore 1994; Mikulincer et al. 2003). There is also evidence of a correlation between the affective valence (i.e. positivity vs. negativity) of input and child ability to attend to the world and to approach challenges — negative affective input correlates with greater child vulnerability to frustration (Volling et al. 2002; Calkins et al. 1998), but so do certain types of positive input such as empty praise (Dweck 1999, 2006, 2007).

In a successful attempt to bridge the two areas of scholarship, Taylor et al. (2009) demonstrated that maternal control strategy varying in power assertion and negative affect mediates the relation between maternal semantic as well as grammatical input and toddlers' pragmatic language development. Specifically, the more negative the mother's control style, the poorer the child's pragmatic performance. But because the study is based on European American subjects, as are most of the studies mentioned in the foregoing paragraph, it remains a question whether the same effect holds across cultures, especially for cultures where the negative maternal control style prevails over the positive control style.

Since there is a large body of literature on cultural differences in parenting style, it would be interesting to find out whether such differences correlate with differences in child pragmatic development across cultures. In an endeavor toward an answer, this chapter explores cultural differences in maternal affective verbal input as the linguistic manifestation of maternal control style or, more globally, parenting style. By affective verbal input I mean child-directed speech acts and utterances that involve a definitive affective valence (positive or negative) for the purpose of influencing the child's behavior. Positive affective input includes praise, thanking, encouragement, and congratulation, while negative affective input includes threat, insult, ridicule, shaming, and criticism. Thus, to expand on Taylor et al. (2009) who primarily focus on affective directives imposed by mothers on their toddlers, I focus on a wider array of affective speech acts because of their relevance and cultural salience.

Theoretically grounded in the ethnography of communication (Gumperz & Hymes 1972; Hymes 1964; Duranti & Goodwin 1992; Duranti 1997; Duranti et al. 2011), I view language as constitutive of everyday social and cultural actions and activities in a speech community, and see social and cultural values, norms, priorities and expectations as relevant to the interpretation of language use. Of particular relevance to this study are works by Ochs and Schieffelin (Ochs 1988, 1989; Schieffelin & Ochs 1986; Ochs & Schieffelin 2011), which cut across language, discourse, affect, and socialization. This study is empirically based and employs both quantitative and qualitative methods. I employ authentic communication data on two cultures drawn from the Child Language Data Exchange System (CHILDES) database: Mandarin Chinese and American English. I seek to answer the following research questions: (1) what kind of affective speech acts are used by mothers to influence child behavior in the two cultures? (2) Are there any consistent cultural patterns in the employment of positive and negative speech acts as social control strategies? (3) What cultural values may account for the observed patterns of maternal pragmatic behavior?

2. Data and methods

The analysis was based on the context-matched American English and Mandarin Chinese corpora of spontaneous mother–child interaction, as detailed in Tardif et al. (1999), retrieved from CHILDES. Both corpora were compiled in the mid

1990s. Each corpus contains transcripts in CHAT format (MacWhinney 1991) from videotapes of 24 mother–child dyads engaged in spontaneous interaction under the same three play conditions: book reading, free play with mechanical toys, and free play with regular toys. The transcripts also include descriptions of the manner in which an utterance is made, such as "softly", "sternly", "laughing", and "whining", which provide valuable non-verbal cues to the affective tendency of the interlocutor. The play materials used for both groups were identical. Each group had 12 girls and 12 boys, with a mean age of 20 months, all normally developing. The children were born to parents of above-average education in the respective societies. The English-speaking mothers and their children were recruited from the research subject pool of a Midwestern university town in the US. The Mandarin-speaking mothers and their children were recruited from hospital immunization records and through word-of-mouth in a university area in Beijing, China. In this study I used 23 transcripts (12 boys, 11 girls) for each language, as in each database there were two transcripts which were apparently recordings of one and the same girl. In each case, a coin was flipped to decide on one of the two transcripts, the other was excluded.

For this study, I identified affective input produced and directed at the toddlers by the mothers, and coded these either as positive or negative. An attitudinal utterance that explicitly expresses approval, admiration, laudation, appreciation, or encouragement counted as a positive affective input. For examples, the following expressions in (1) from the American English corpus were counted as positive affective input:

(1)   *Good girl/boy!*
      Good job!
      That's great.
      Thank you!
      You can do it!

The examples in (2) illustrate positive affective input in Mandarin Chinese:

(2)   *Hao haizi!* ('Good child!')
      Zhen hao! ('Great!')
      Zhen bang! ('Awesome!')
      Zhen nenggan. ('You're so capable!')
      Tai hao le. ('Very good!')

An attitudinal utterance that explicitly expresses disapproval, disdain, derision, or criticism, or directly berates or threatens the addressee counted as a negative affective input. For examples, the following Chinese expressions in (3) were counted as negative affective input:

(3) *Ni zenme zheme butinghua!* ('How disobedient you are!')
     Huai si-le! ('You're so bad!')
     Mama shengqi le. ('Mommy is getting mad at you.')
     Wo zou ni! ('I'll spank you!')
     Zhen ben. ('You're stupid.')
     Mei chu-xi! ('You're good for nothing!')

As we will see in the analysis, there are very few negative affective expressions in the American data. Besides, the few negative expressions are qualitatively different from the Chinese ones. Consider the following American examples:

(4) *You are grumpy.*
     Don't be grumpy.
     You get time out if you do that.

Compared with the speech acts in (3), the expressions in (4) pertain matter-of-factly to a temporary state of affairs rather than a permanent trait. This temporariness is true of the characterization of the child's current mood state, the rejection of that state, and the threat of a punishment. In annotating the data, I did not count the playfully negative utterance *you're (being) silly* as a negative affective speech act unless the mother's manner is explicitly coded as "stern" in the transcript. The very playfulness of the expression serves to reverse or minimize the negativity of the mother's input.[1]

Non-attitudinal expressions that objectively judge the correctness or incorrectness of an answer to a question asked by the mother were not counted as affective speech acts, such as *no, that's not red/a bunny* or *that's right* and its Mandarin Chinese counterpart *dui* 'right'. Non-attitudinal speech acts that tell whether a child is allowed or disallowed to do something, e.g. *no, you can't tear the book* or *don't pull/break the toy* and their Mandarin Chinese counterparts were not counted as affective speech acts unless the mother's manner is coded as "stern" in the transcript. Positive comments on the toys were also excluded from the analysis.

Two quantitative analyses were conducted. First, a *t* test was conducted comparing the two groups in terms of the means of their positive and negative affective input. This analysis was based on the relative frequencies of affective speech acts per 1000 utterances rather than raw token frequencies for the analysis for both corpora. This is because the number of total maternal utterances varies from dyad to dyad and across languages. The number of total maternal utterances in one dyadic interaction ranges from 359 to 926 with a mean of 585 in the American corpus. The range is from 420 to 1064 with a mean of 770 in the Mandarin corpus.

---

1. In some of the instances, coding of the mother's paralinguistic cues such as laughing provides extra evidence of playfulness.

The two groups were compared and contrasted with regard to the mean relative frequencies of positive and negative affective speech acts. Second, a chi-squared test for independence was conducted to test whether or not the maternal input patterns are related to culture (that is, being American or Chinese). The null hypothesis is that the maternal input patterns are unrelated to culture.

3.   Results

3.1   American maternal positivity vs. Chinese maternal negativity

The results on the mean frequencies of positive versus negative maternal affective input in the Chinese and the American sample are presented in Figure 1. The t test revealed a statistically significant difference between mean frequency of positive affective input by the American mothers (M = 17.6513, SD = 12.67693) and the Chinese mothers (M = 7.0957, SD = 8.30904), t (44) = 3.34, p = .002, α = .05, as well as a statistically reliable difference between the mean frequency of negative affective input by American mothers (M = .4352, SD = 1.04143) and Chinese mothers (M = 8.7361, SD = 13.11829), t (22.277) = 3.025, p = .006, α = .05. The data indicate that on average American mothers give their children significantly more positive affective input than Chinese mothers, and that on average Chinese mothers give their children significantly more negative affective input than American mothers.

However, by comparing the means of the two groups, the t test only reveals the global difference between the two groups in their average amount of positive and negative input, but does not show the extent to which the issuance and

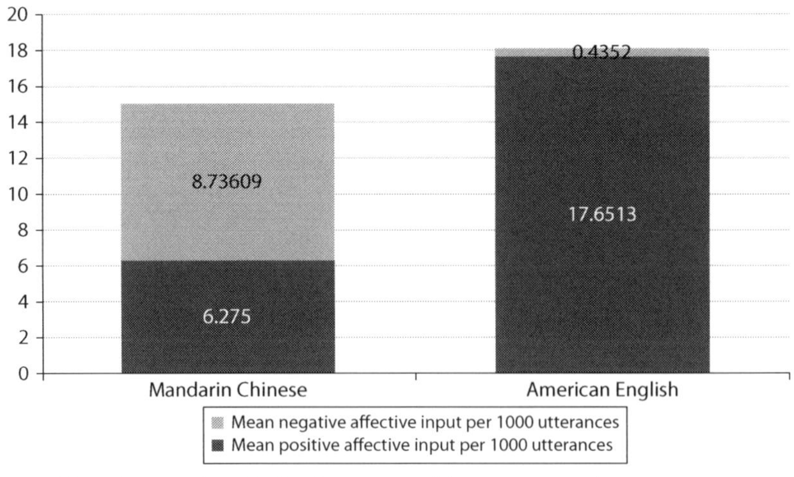

Figure 1. Mean frequencies of affective maternal input across cultures

Table 1. Culture versus positive and negative affective input

Input type		Positive			Negative		
		yes	no	Total	yes	no	Total
Culture	American English	23	0	23	4	19	23
	Mandarin Chinese	19	4	23	20	3	23
Total				46			46

non-issuance of each type of input by the mothers is related to culture rather than a matter of individual choice. To investigate this, I counted for each group the number of mothers that did and did not issue any positive input, and the number of mothers that did and did not issue any negative input, as shown in Table 1.

The chi-squared test of independence between culture and the issuance of each type of input revealed a statistically significant impact of culture on the issuance of positive input ($X^2(1) = 4.381$, $p = .036$) at the alpha level of .05., and a very significant impact of culture on the issuance of negative input ($X^2(1) = 22.303$, $p < .0001$). Therefore, the null hypothesis that the patterns of affective maternal input are unrelated to culture is rejected. These results, together with the t test results, suggest that the mothers in the two groups behave differently in giving affective input to their children, and the differences are culturally significant. In what follows, I will examine the positive and negative affective input in the two samples by looking at the types of positive and negative speech acts in turn.

3.2 Praise and appreciation — Positive maternal affective input

There is another way to look at the numbers in Figure 1 in 3.1. On average, in any given 1000 utterances, American mothers utter 40.56 positive affective speech acts for every one negative affective speech act. By contrast, for every one negative affective speech act, Chinese mothers give less than one (0.7) positive speech act. This contrast is very telling and suggests that the average amount of verbal rewards in the American data is disproportionally bigger than that in the Chinese data. But what is behind the number is equally revealing about how the two groups of mothers use affective language use in child-directed communication.

When we look at positive affective input from a qualitative perspective, we may notice a seeming commonality between American and Chinese mothers: both praise their children. A close examination of the types of praise and the contexts in which praise is issued by the two groups of mothers, however, reveals a more complicated picture. First, the praises issued by mothers in both cultures mainly fall into two types: Person Praise and Outcome Praise. Following Kamins and Dweck (1999), praise can be classified into Person Praise, Process Praise, and Outcome

Praise, which refer respectively to praise of the child as a person or the child's personal characteristics, praise of the child's methods of approaching a task or activity, and praise of the child's accomplishments in carrying out a task or activity. Person Praise is more general and global than Outcome Praise and Process Praise because it is not specific to an action or event. Typical instances of Person Praise in the American data are *good girl, that's a big girl* and *good boy*, and typical instances of Person Praise in the Mandarin data include *hao haizi* 'Good child', *hao baobao* 'Good baby', *XX* (name of child) *zhen guai* 'XX is so good/well-behaved', *XX zhen congming* 'XX is really smart', and *XX zhen bang* 'XX is so awesome'. Typical instances of Outcome Praise in the American data are *good job, that was great*, and *didn't it feel good that you could do it* and typical instances of Outcome Praise in the Chinese data are *zhen hao* 'great' and *tai hao le* 'very good'.

Second, American mothers issue praise, either Person or Outcome Praise, directly in response to their children's task-based accomplishments. Chinese mothers, on the other hand, use praise both as a reward in response to their children's accomplishments, and as a tool of behavioral manipulation to get their children to do something they deem desirable. For example, consider the praises underlined in the sequences in (5) and (6) as illustrations of praise as reward and praise as behavioral manipulation, respectively:

(5)   Praise as reward of accomplishments
      American English

```
*MOT:   <where's the green one> [=! whisper] ?
%mor:   adv:wh|where~v:cop|be&3S det|the adj|green pro:indef|one?
%gra:   1|2|PRED 2|0|ROOT 3|5|DET 4|5|MOD 5|2|SUBJ 6|2|PUNCT
%com:   4 second pause .
*MOT:   good girl (.) yeah Lindz !
%mor:   adj|good n|girl co|yeah n:prop|Lindz !
%gra:   1|2|MOD 2|0|ROOT 3|4|COM 4|2|VOC 5|2|PUNCT
*CHI:   0 [% quick breath] .
%com:   blocks fall .
*CHI:   &uh !
*MOT:   try it again .
%mor:   v|try pro|it adv|again .
%gra:   1|0|ROOT 2|1|OBJ 3|1|JCT 4|1|PUNCT
%com:   2 seconds of blocks falling .
*MOT:   you're doing a good job, honey .
```

      Mandarin Chinese

```
*MOT:   zhei4 shi4 hu2die2 .
*MOT:   hu2die2 (.) shi4 shen2me yan2se4 de ya ?
```

```
%cod:   $Q:QW
*CHI:   lan2 da .
*MOT:   dui4 la (1.) .
*MOT:   zhen1 hao3 (1.) .
```

Translation
Mother: This is a butterfly.
Mother: What color is the butterfly?
Child: Blue.
Mother: Right.
Mother: <u>Very good.</u>

(6)   *Praise as behavioral manipulation*
     Mandarin Chinese

```
*MOT:   zuo4hao3 (.) zuo4hao3 .
*MOT:   lai2 .
*MOT:   lai2 zuo4hao3 .
*CHI:   <shu1zi> [>] .
*MOT:   <lai2 ting2ting ke3> [<] ting1hua4 la .

*MOT:   na4 ni3 bie2 neng4 +…
*MOT:   bie2 wanr2 nei4ge hao3 ma ?
%cod:   $Q:QP:T
*MOT:   lai2 zuo4hao3 .
*MOT:   ting2ting ke3 guai1 le .
```

Translation
Mother: Sit down. Sit down.
Mother: Come here.
Mother: Come and sit down.
Child: A comb.
Mother: <u>Come here, Tingting is very obedient.</u>

Mother: Don't do that …
Mother: Don't play with that, okay?
Mother: Come and sit down.
Mother: <u>Tingting is so well-behaved.</u>

The praises given by American and Chinese mothers in (5) are appetitive stimuli in response to the child's successful attempt at a task. In (6), however, the two praises are not given to the child because of something she has succeeded in doing. They are given to the child because she is not doing what the mother is directing her to do, and the mother attempts to manipulate the child into complying with the maternal request by employing praises of anticipated obedience to prevent potential defiant behavior. I call this kind of praise "anticipatory praise", a type found in the Chinese, but not the American data.

Third, unlike American mothers, Chinese mothers often issue praises of obedience and good behavior in response to their children's task-based accomplishments. That is, the child's success in carrying out a task is taken by the mother as a token of his/her obedience and good behavior, for which the mother gives praise. The accomplishment per se is not the object of praise. Consider (7) as an example:

```
(7)  *MOT:   wang3qian2fan1 .
     *CHI:   <&e:mmn:> [>] < (1.) > [<] .
     %cod:   $UNINT
     *MOT:   <xi1xi1> [>] zi4ji3 fan1 .
     *MOT:   kan4kan4 xi1xi1 fan1 de hao3 zhe ne .
     *MOT:   xi1xi1 .
     %cod:   $VOC
     *MOT:   xi1xi1 cai2 guai1 .
     *CHI:   +^ duo1duo1 [: deng4deng4] [*] .
     *MOT:   xi1xi1 <zui4 ting1hua4 le> [<] .
```

Translation
Mother: Turn the page.
Child: Hm.
Mother: Turn the page by yourself.
Mother: Look how nicely Xixi is turning the page.
Mother: Xixi.
Mother: Xixi is so well-behaved.
Child: A stool.
Mother: Xixi is the most obedient of all.

In (7), the mother's first praise expresses admiration of the child's accomplishment. However, the second and the third are both generic praises of the child's obedience and good behavior, which is presumably reflected in her success in carrying out the task of turning the page. Thus, it seems that the mother's positive affective input is not just about what the child does and how successful the child is in doing it during one particular play event; it is more about the child's fulfilled role as a subordinate in the dyadic relationship.

Fourth, American mothers, but not Chinese mothers, praise their children for hard work, which exemplifies Process Praise. That is, rather than emphasizing a permanent trait, e.g. goodness or intelligence, or the final result of an action, the mothers focus on the means or process by which the child works to accomplish something. Consider (8) as an example:

```
(8)  *CHI:   &uh [=! whining] .
     *MOT:   &aw, you get kinda [: kind of] frustrated when it falls
     over ?
     %mor:   pro|you v|get adj|kind prep|of part|frustrate-PERF
     conj:subor|when pro|it v|fall-3S adv:loc|over ?
     %gra:   1|2|SUBJ 2|0|ROOT 3|2|PRED 4|3|MOD 5|4|POBJ 6|8|CPZR
     7|8|SUBJ 8|2|CJCT 9|8|JCT 10|2|PUNCT
     %com:   3 sec pause
     *MOT:   you're working very hard: to just stand that up .
```

In this scene, the child is attempting to make a block stand up, which seems to be a tricky task that causes the child to whine in frustration. The mother, however, captures the moment as an opportunity to praise the child for trying and working hard.

Fifth, as far as positive affective input is concerned, what distinguishes American mothers from Chinese mothers is as much the praise they lavish on their children as the appreciations they freely express. Out of a total of 236 positive speech acts in the American data, 65 (27.54%) are expressions of appreciation, given by 17 (73.91%) out of 23 mothers. Consider the following example in (9):

```
(9)  *MOT:   can you dance ?
     %mor:   aux|can pro|you v|dance ?
     %gra:   1|3|AUX 2|3|SUBJ 3|0|ROOT 4|3|PUNCT
     *MOT:   you wanna dance ?
     %mor:   pro|you v|want~inf|to v|dance ?
     %gra:   1|2|SUBJ 2|0|ROOT 3|4|INF 4|2|XCOMP 5|2|PUNCT
     %com:   music for 16 sec
     *MOT:   thank+you .
     *MOT:   you found if ?
     %mor:   pro|you v|find&PAST conj:subor|if ?
     %gra:   1|2|SUBJ 2|0|ROOT 3|2|OBJ 4|2|PUNCT
     *MOT:   thanks Martin .
     %mor:   co|thanks n:prop|Martin .
     %gra:   1|2|COM 2|0|ROOT 3|2|PUNCT
     *MOT:   thank+you .
```

The fact that American mothers thank their children for their actions during the interaction suggests that they frame the mother–child relationship as one of reciprocity in which there is giving and taking, and appreciation is expressed for a favor done. By contrast, there is only one (0.81%) instance of thanking in the entire Chinese database of 124 positive affective speech acts. This one instance, I shall quickly add, is expressed not directly by the mother, but in the voice of a toy animal, as in (10), where the mother is asking the child to pick up stuffed animals:

```
(10)  *MOT:   zai4jian3 a .
      *MOT:   a (.) nei4 shi4 gou3gou3 .
      *MOT:   dui4 .
      *MOT:   xiao3 xiong2 jian3qi3lai2 .
      *MOT:   &ai .
      %cod:   $INTERJ
      *MOT:   xiao3 tu4tu4 .
      *MOT:   xie4xie4 tao2tao gelge .
```

Translation
Mother: Pick up some more.
Mother: Ah, that's a doggie.
Mother: Right.
Mother: Pick up the teddy.
Mother: Aha.
Mother: Little bunny.
Mother: Thank you older brother Taotao.

In the last utterance above, the mother is speaking through the little bunny. In an enactment of appreciation, the bunny calls the child "older brother" and thanks him. Apart from this instance, no appreciation is communicated to a child by any of the Chinese mothers.

3.3 Threatening, scolding, and name-calling — Negative maternal affective input

The data in 3.1 show that American mothers generally avoid negative affective input in interaction with their children; but Chinese mothers freely employ negative input. The difference is not only quantitative, the two datasets differ qualitatively, too, to which we will now turn.

A total of seven negative speech acts, uttered by 4 mothers, were identified in the entire American English data. Out of these, three are conditional sentences expressing a threat contingent on the child's failure to comply with the mother, e.g. *you get time out if you do that*. Three are copula sentences with an adjectival/gerundive predicative, characterizing a temporary negative state the child is in, e.g. *you're grumpy*. One is a negative imperative forbidding the child from being "grumpy" — *don't be grumpy*. Consider the following interaction as an example:

```
(11)  *MOT:   let's look at the book .
      *CHI:   no: [=! whining and crying] .
      *MOT:   don't xxx .
      %com:   child cries
```

```
*MOT:   hey .
*CHI:   no: [=! whining] .
*MOT:   yes .
*MOT:   &ah, what's that ?
*CHI:   no: [=! crying] .
*MOT:   what is that ?
*CHI:   no: [=! crying] .
*MOT:   don't be grumpy .
```

In this sequence, the mother attempts to engage the child in the book reading activity. The child refuses to cooperate by whining and crying and repeatedly saying "no". The mother delivers the negative imperative in response to the child's behavior. Note that the word "grumpy" carries a negative evaluation of what it describes and distinguishes the negative imperative from a more neutral "stop crying". However, it is still situation-bound and pertains to a temporary state of mood.

In the Chinese data, 20 out of 23 mothers produced a total of 155 negative speech acts. These Chinese mothers' negative affective input generally includes threatening (37.42%) in the form of a conditional sentence, scolding (57.42%) in the form of a subject-predicate clause with adjectival or verbal predicate, and name-calling (8%) in the form of a noun phrase, which either stands on its own or serves as the nominal predicative of a copula clause. While threatening is used as a device of social control by both groups, the scope of usage is dramatically different between the two groups. Two (8.7%) mothers use threatening in the American data, but 19 (i.e. 82.61% of all the Chinese mothers, and 95% of all the Chinese mothers who gave negative input) mothers resort to threatening in the Chinese data. This difference suggests the sporadic nature of the use of threat as an individual phenomenon in the American group, in stark contrast to the pervasiveness of this type of negative speech act in the Chinese group. The large scope of usage identified in the Mandarin data converges with a previous finding that Chinese mothers' socio-economic background as measured by education is not a predictor of the usage of threatening speech acts. Blue collar and professional mothers are equally likely to threaten their children verbally (Jing-Schmidt 2009). The result is also consistent with Zhou and Jin's (this volume) finding that Chinese mothers' education background has no effect on their child-directed communication patterns at the socio-pragmatic level, although it makes a difference in terms of the frequency of input, utterance length, and vocabulary size.

Furthermore, the Chinese mothers' threatening input is fundamentally different from its American counterpart in that a threat is issued not just as a hypothetical punishment but, more importantly, to evoke guilt in the child. Thus, while American mothers' threats are strictly behavior-oriented, Chinese mothers' threats can often be emotion-oriented. Consider (12)–(14):

(12)   *MOT: na4 ni3 chuan1shang4 xie2 ba .
       *MOT: bu4 xu3 !
       *MOT: bu4 xu3 zhei4yang4 xia4di4 le a: .
       *MOT: bu4 xu3 guang1 zhe jiao3 xia4di4 le (.) .
       *MOT: <u>ni3 zai4 guang1 zhe jiao3 xia4di4 ma1ma zou4 ni3 (.) .</u>
       *MOT: lai2 (.) chuan1shang4 xie2 (2.) .
       *MOT: chuan1shang4 yi4zhi xie2 a: .
       *MOT: jiu4 bu4 xu3 xia4di4 le a: (4.) .
       *MOT: <u>ni3 zai4 xia4di4 (1.) ma1ma jiu (1.) sheng1qi4 le .</u>
       *MOT: <u>ma1ma sheng1qi4 le a .</u>

Translation
Mother: Put on your shoes then.
Mother: Don't!
Mother: Don't go down like this.
Mother: Don't go down bare-footed.
<u>Mother: Mommy will beat you if you go bare foot again.</u>
Mother: Come on, put on your shoes.
Mother: Put on a shoe.
Mother: You don't go bare foot.
<u>Mother: If you go again, mommy will get mad at you.</u>
<u>Mother: Mommy is getting mad at you.</u>

(13)   *MOT: wen4wen4 xiao3 ya1zi .
       *MOT: ni3 shuo1 (.) ni3 zen3me le ?
       %cod: $Q:QW
       *CHI: xiao3 ya1: .
       *MOT: xiao3 ya1zi shuo1 .
       *MOT: <u>bei4bei4 bu4 gen1 wo3 wanr2 .</u>
       *MOT: <u>wo3 sheng1qi4 le .</u>

Translation
Mother: Ask the duckling.
Mother: Say what's the matter with you?
Child: Duckling.
Mother: Duckling says.
<u>Mother: Beibei doesn't play with me.</u>
<u>Mother: I am getting mad.</u>

(14)   *MOT: zher4 shi4 shen2me (3.) ?
       %cod: $Q:QW
       *MOT: ni3 you4 bu4 hao3hao3 xue2 le (.) shi4 bu4 shi4 ?
       %cod: $Q:VNV:T
       *MOT: <u>ma1ma bu4 gen1 ni3 hao3 le a: .</u>

Translation
Mother: What's this?
Mother: You're not learning nicely, are you?
<u>Mother: Mommy will stop loving you.</u>

In (12), the mother threatens the child three times. The first threat poses a hypothetical physical punishment. The subsequent two threats pertain to the possible world in which the mother gets angry with the child and their relationship is jeopardized. Note that behind this anger threat, there is an assumption that the child is responsible for the mother's emotion, and therefore if the mother gets angry, it is the child's fault. In (13), the same guilt-inducing threatening strategy is employed by the mother, only this time it is expressed through the personified voice of a toy duckling, with which the child would not play. The threat in (14) proposes a withdrawal of maternal affection. Out of a total of 58 instances of threatening in the Chinese data, 18 instances (31.03%) are emotion-oriented.

Chinese mothers may also use threatening as a general device of deterrence without targeting a particular misbehavior. Consider (15) below:

```
(15)  *MOT:   ni3 kan4 zhei4 da4 lao3shu3 (1.) .
      *MOT:   pa4 bu2 pa4 (1.) ?
      %cod:   $Q:VNV
      *MOT:   pa4 bu4 pa4 ?
      %cod:   $Q:VNV
      *CHI:   pa4 .
      *MOT:   &a: .
      %cod:   $INTERJ
      *MOT:   na4 ni3 yao4 tao2qi4 (.) da4 lao3shu3 (1.) .
      *MOT:   yao3 bu4 yao3 ni3 ya (.) ?
      %cod:   $Q:VNV
      *CHI:   &yiya .
      %cod:   $UNINT
      *MOT:   da4 lao3shu3 yao3 bu4 yao3 ren2 ya ?
```

Translation
Mother: Look at this big rat.
Mother: Are you afraid of it?
Mother: Are you afraid?
Child: (Yes, I'm) afraid.
Mother: Ah.
<u>Mother: So if you are naughty, will the big rat</u>
<u>Mother: bite you or not?</u>
Child: Yiya.
Mother: Do big rats bite or not?

In this case, the absurdity of the threat that the big rat (in the picture book) might come off the page and bite the child may seem obvious to many. Yet the fact that the mother, during the book reading activity, is capable of conjuring up that scenario as a looming danger hypothesized on the condition of the child's eventual naughty behavior is revealing of the deep entrenchment of threatening as a conventional tool of social control. The use of threatening by Chinese mothers can indeed reach a level of creativity unseen elsewhere in mother–child interaction. Witness (16), another book reading sequence involving a different mother–child pair:

```
(16)  *MOT:   < ni3 bu2 kan4shu1 la > [>] .
      *CHI:   &a: [!] [<] .
      %cod:   $INTERJ
      *CHI:   &a: .
      %cod:   $INTERJ
      *MOT:   you (.) yihuir3 da4 shi1zi lai2 le .
      *MOT:   ni3 kan4 nar4 you3 mei2you3 shi1zi a ?
      %cod:   $Q:VNV
      *MOT:   ni3 yi2 jiao4 shi1zi jiu4 gai1 lai2 le .
      *MOT:   yao3 ni3 lai2 le jiu4 .
      *MOT:   ni3 kan4 a .
      *MOT:   di4 yilye4 jin4 shi4 da4 shi1zi .
      *MOT:   ni3 kan4 da4 shi1zi li4hai4 ba .
```

Translation
Mother: You don't want to look at the book anymore?
Child: A! (No, I don't.)
Child: A.
Mother: Oh, the big lion is coming shortly.
Mother: Look, is there a lion there or not?
Mother: If you shout the lion will come.
Mother: It will come to bite you.
Mother: Look it.
Mother: The whole first (page) is a big lion.
Mother: You see the big lion is ferocious.

In this sequence, the mother seems to be attempting to redirect the child's attention to the book in which the child shows no interest. The mother appears to have a natural understanding that fear is a potent attention-getter, and utilizes it in order to get the child to look at the book. It is clear from (15) and (16) that Chinese mothers can draw on a variety of potential fear stimuli and create an instant scenario of threat in their interaction with the child.

On another occasion, a Chinese mother warns her toddler of the potential danger of ending up being inferior to his peers if he misses a chance for learning, as in (17).

(17) *MOT: zan2men zai4 kan4 yi2bian4 .
      *MOT: hao3 bu4 hao3 ?
      %cod: $Q:VNV
      *MOT: ni3 xue2 yi4dianr3 .
      *MOT: bie2ren2 dou1 hui4 de .
      *MOT: ni3 jiu4 bu2 hui4 le .

Translation
Mother: Let's look at it one more time.
Mother: Is that all right?
Mother: You learn a little bit.
Mother: (Otherwise) everyone else knows it.
Mother: You'll be the only one who doesn't.

Here, the Chinese mother is asking her 20 month old to learn from the picture book, which she suggests they read one more time. By pointing out a looming negative consequence of non-compliance, namely the child's eventual inferiority to his peers in terms of competitiveness, the mother raises the child's awareness of competition and the consequent shame of losing. Although the mother's utterances in (17) are not explicitly negative, they invite a negative inference that puts the child in an unpleasant light, which no doubt has affective consequences for the child. From this example, it is not hard to infer the prominent place of competition in the culture and the value of academic success to Chinese parents.

Chinese mothers' scolding is also qualitatively distinct in two respects. First, a Chinese mother's scolding tends to frame the object of criticism as a permanent trait — either the child's general personal quality or a habitual tendency, rather than focusing on an instantaneous misbehavior or a current state of being. Second, a Chinese mother's scolding ignores the child's feelings and disregards the child's dignity and self-determination. Consider (18) and (19), below:

(18) *MOT: shen2me yan2se4 ?
      %cod: $Q:QW
      *CHI: feng1che1 .
      *MOT: tao3yan4 .
      *MOT: zhei4 shi4 shen2me ?
      %cod: $Q:QW
      *CHI: niao3: .
      *MOT: ha (.) zhei4ge shi4 niao3 .
      *MOT: nen4 hui4 ting1hua4 (.) .

Translation
Mother: What color is this?
Child: Windmill.
Mother: Obnoxious.
Mother: What's this?
Child: bird.
Mother: Hm, this is a bird.
Mother: So disobedient.

(19) *MOT: eiyou: (.) zhei4ge shen2me ya ?
      %cod: $Q:QW
      *CHI: kan4 bu4 qing1 .
      *MOT: hu2shuo1 [!] zhei4 shi4 shen2me ?

Translation
Mother: Oh, what's this?
Child: Can't see it clearly.
Mother: Nonsense! What's this?

In (18), the mother calls her child 'obnoxious' because the child fails to answer her question correctly. The mother is so annoyed by this failure that she carries the negative emotion over to the subsequent interaction and calls the child 'disobedient' despite the fact that the child correctly answers the question this time. The child's instant failure to accomplish a task apparently is met with severe scolding tinged with hostility and disrespect. This example also illustrates Chinese mothers' insistence on prompt filial obedience. In fact, 19 (21.35%) out of 89 scolding instances are about disobedience. In (19), the child's answer obviously fails to please the mother who expects a quicker response. As a result, the mother abruptly dismisses the answer altogether as 'nonsense', apparently showing little respect for the child. Compared with the matter-of-fact quality of American mothers' criticism, the Chinese mothers' input is laden with negative emotions such as disgust and anger.

Name-calling is a form of negative speech act packaged in a lexicalized noun phrase that labels a person or a certain characteristic of a person. This type of negative input is observed in the Chinese, but not the American data where the only item that formally resembles a label is *silly goose*. However, as explained previously, the playfulness inherent in this phrase tells us that it is used for fun and humor instead of as a put-down. The following examples illustrate maternal name-calling in Mandarin Chinese:

(20) *MOT: zhei4 shi4 shen2me ?
      %cod: $Q:QW
      *CHI: qiu2 .

```
*CHI:    &cha .
%cod:    $UNINT
*MOT:    sha3gua1danr4 .
```

Translation
Mother: What's this?
Child: Ball.
Child: xxx (unintelligible)
Mother: Blockhead.

```
(21)  *MOT:    gai4 nei4 da4 gao1 lou2 .
      *MOT:    hao3 bu4 hao3 (.) ?
      %cod:    $Q:VNV
      *MOT:    ni3 shuo1 hao3 (2.) .
      *MOT:    kan4 zhe a: (2.) .
      *MOT:    xx gei3 xi1xi1 kai4ge da4 gao1 lou2 (5.) .
      *CHI:    &ya (2.) .
      %cod:    $UNINT
      *MOT:    nong4 [?] dao3 a: (1.) ?
      %cod:    $Q:NQP
      *MOT:    ni3 zen3me nen4me huai4 a (.) ni3 (.) ?
      %cod:    $Q:QW
      *MOT:    xiao3 huai4bao1 (5.) .
```

Translation
Mother: Let's build a big building.
Mother: Is that good?
Mother: You say good.
Mother: Look.
Mother: (I'm) building a big building for Xixi.
Child: Oh.
Mother: You're knocking it over?
Mother: Why are you so wicked?
Mother: Little villain (Lit. 'little evil bundle').

The consequences of name-calling can be looked at in many different ways. From a
grammatical perspective, parts of speech have cognitive consequences. Langacker
(1987) argues that nouns denote entities which are by definition time-stable and
absolute. This view has been confirmed by research on the effect of labeling. In an
experiment by Gelman and Hayman (1999), five and seven years old children were
given a verbal characterization of a fictitious character. For each character, half the
children heard a description with a nominal predicate (e.g. *She is a carrot-eater*),
and half heard a verbal predicate (*She eats carrots whenever she can*). The children

judged a characteristic as more stable over time and across contexts when described by a lexicalized noun phrase than when described by a verbal predicate. This finding has implications for our study of name-calling, as it allows the inference that name-calling has more stable and long-lasting impact than non-nominal expressions by virtue of its part of speech. That is, the Chinese mothers' name-calling may inadvertently perpetuate a characteristic because of the stable and long-lasting impact it has as a nominal category. It is true that some forms of name-calling may appear playful and amusing, and may not be intended as insult. There is no denying that when using negative language, Chinese mothers attempt to teach, to socialize values, and to motivate their children. But means and end must not be confused, and maternal affective input is worth studying precisely because there is a distinction between means and end. Whether or not end justifies means is a completely different issue, which everyone is free to decide for themselves.

In summary of the above analysis, it is clear that American mothers rarely resort to negative affective input in their interaction with their children. Chinese mothers, on the other hand, are generally uninhibited in their employment of threatening, scolding, and name-calling. Furthermore, there are two features specific to the Chinese data. One is emotion-oriented verbal threatening involving, for example, hypothetical anger directed at a child or withdrawal of love from the child. The other feature is that Chinese mothers insist on the child's obedience and consistently scold the child for being disobedient or defiant.

These results could easily lead to a conclusion that Chinese mothers are "authoritarian" and perhaps "unloving", "hostile", or even "abusive". However, as Chao (1994) argues, the concepts of "control" and "authoritarian" parenting have completely different meanings and implications in American and Chinese cultural context. The intention and motivation behind the Chinese maternal behavior are also very different from that of typical authoritarian parents in the American context. Chao asserts that Chinese mothers control their children in accordance with the cultural expectation of "training" and "governance" of the child, which are associated with concern, care and involvement.[2] In fact, as Chao's data demonstrate, not only are views of ideal parenting practices culturally specific, but also maternal love itself is culturally defined. Compared with European American mothers, Chinese American mothers are significantly more likely to strongly endorse a view of love as primarily expressed by maternal involvement and close supervision, and in particular helping the child to succeed in school. Therefore, the consideration of culture as a conditioning factor of parenting and maternal communication style is necessary for an adequate interpretation of the data.

---

2. The native concepts invoked by Chao are *chiao shun (jiaoxun)* 'training' and *guan* 'governance', respectively.

4. Discussion

The patterns of language use by American mothers in interaction with their children reveal a strong positivity bias characterized by the predominance of praise and appreciation, and a scarcity of negativity. The patterns of language use by Chinese mothers point to a prevalence of negativity, an emphasis on obedience, habitual overgeneralization of personality, and the significance of guilt in the mother–child relationship. The findings are consistent with available knowledge of cultural differences between Americans and East Asians in parenting approaches in general (Miller, Wiley, Fung & Liang 1997, Miller, Wang, Sandel & Cho 2002), and how parents respond to their children's performance in particular (Ng et al. 2007). While American parents tend to see their children's behavior in a positive light, thereby highlighting their successes and downplaying their failures, East Asian parents tend to pay more attention to their children's failures and understate their successes. The findings are also consistent with available documentations of cultural differences between Americans and East Asians in their self-evaluation with regard to success and failure. Generally, the "self-enhancement" tendency is stronger among North Americans than among East Asians who view failure as more salient and more relevant to self-improvement than success (Heine, Lehman, Markus & Kitayama 1999; Heine, Kitayama, & Lehman 2001, Heine 2005; see Heine & Hamamura 2007 for a review).

In addition to the negativity bias, Chinese mothers' positive input is also different from that of their American counterparts. First, on average, they give the children fewer praises than American mothers. Some may assume that because Chinese mothers praise their children infrequently, their praise will be highly valued if it is ever given to a child. Tempting as this assumption may be, it fails to recognize that it is the nature of praise that matters in how it is perceived by children. If praise is specific to an episode, it is likely to be valued by children because they realize that they have "earned" it. By contrast, an empty generic praise is unlikely to be valued by children because they know they have done nothing to "earn" the praise (Kohn 2001). Thus, one must withhold the simplistic judgment that infrequent praise is more beneficial than frequent praise by virtue of its sheer rarity. Second, instead of praising what the children do and accomplish, Chinese mothers tend to praise the children's obedience, sometimes for the purpose of preventing potential defiance. This tendency is in line with the cultural value placed on filial obedience. Third, while American mothers freely express appreciation for what their children do, Chinese mothers almost never say *thank you* to their children.

The parenting styles in the two cultures in general and the differential biases exhibited in American and Chinese maternal speech acts in particular cannot be accounted for without reference to the conceptualization of the mother–child relationship as shaped by culture-specific ideologies and philosophies, and the consequent differing cultural preoccupations, priorities, and practices (Belsky 1980, 1984; Bronfenbrenner 1977; Hinde 1979; Hinde & Stevenson-Hinde 1987; Patterson 1982). On the one hand, I will focus on the cultural emphasis on positive reinforcement as an educational and therapeutic strategy motivated by the self-esteem movement in American social psychology. On the other hand, I will discuss the Confucian doctrine of parental authority and the worship of learning in the Chinese culture. I consider these factors for their cultural salience in providing background in which to understand the cultural patterns we observe in the maternal affective input, and the parenting styles behind those patterns. I hasten to acknowledge though that both cultures are far richer and more complicated than these particular ideologies and philosophies would seem to imply.

The American psychologist Abraham Maslow (1943, 1954) proposed a theory of human motivation, arguing that the actualization of one's full potential is the final step of optimal human development. To accomplish self-actualization, he maintained, the foundation and key motivating force is self-esteem. Following this theory, subsequent scholars and educators attempted to identify the instrument to building self-esteem and strengthening motivation, and believed to have found it in positive reinforcement (Brandon 1969). Positive reinforcement is defined as the adding of an appetitive stimulus to increase a certain behavior or response (Azrin & Holz 1966), a central idea in behaviorism (Skinner 1970). The decades that followed saw the publication of academic papers (Strain et al. 1984; Strain & Kohler 1998; Webster-Stratton 1999; Wolery 2000; Odem & Strain 2002) in favor of positive reinforcements. A society where individualism is highly valued naturally resonates with and provides a seedbed for a movement that promotes self-esteem.

Unsurprisingly, over the years, parenting and educational methods aimed to boost self-esteem were advocated and recommended by experts and practiced by teachers and parents with such enthusiasm that it is no exaggeration to say that American educational culture has become synonymous with the culture of praise (Kohn 2001). By the 1980s, efforts were made in schools nationally to increase children's self-esteem (Twenge & Campbell 2001; Twenge 2006). Twenge and her colleagues (Twenge et al. 2008b: 925) sum up the scope of "self-esteem programs" in the U.S. by observing that "Americans are administering a psychological intervention to an entire population of children when only a small minority shows any sign of needing it." American mothers responded to the changing trend in parenting and all agreed on the importance of boosting children's self-esteem (Cho et al. 2005).[3] In view of the fervor surrounding self-esteem, one can hardly disagree

---

3. This same study found the opposite attitude among Mandarin speaking Taiwanese mothers who did not think it is particularly important to boost the children's self-esteem.

with Baumeister and his colleagues (Baumeister et al. 2003: 1) who note that "self-esteem has become a household word", and that self-esteem has been embraced as a "social panacea" in the U.S.

Under the influence of this cultural emphasis on self-esteem, the role of the mother in the mother–child dyad is conceptualized as one of a facilitative nature. In other words, the mother is expected to boost the child's self-esteem, thereby supporting the child's self-actualization. In light of the conventionalization and cultural significance of positive reinforcements in the U.S., it comes as no surprise that American mothers' affective verbal input is overwhelmingly positive while negative input is the exception. When mothers praise their children, they are making an attempt to fulfill the culturally prescribed role as the principal provider of positive reinforcements, and the principal builder of their children's self-esteem.

Of course, the pedagogical meaningfulness of self-esteem and positive reinforcement demands empirical testing. Recent empirical research in social psychology has not found evidence that boosting self-esteem reliably produces long-term benefits with the possible exception of happiness; rather, self-esteem may be more plausibly interpreted as the effect of social and academic success (Baumeister et al. 2003). Meanwhile, there is experimental evidence that some forms of praise can be more harmful than helpful (Dweck 1999, 2006, 2007; Cimpian et al. 2007). On the other hand, a nationwide generational meta-analysis showed a 30% increase of narcissism level among American college students who completed the Narcissistic Personality Inventory between 1979 and 2006. The emergence of the "generation me", to use Twenge's (2006) term, is a likely sign of the backlash against an educational approach driven by self-esteem.[4]

When it comes to Chinese culture, two traditional concepts are deeply entrenched in the collective unconscious and remain influential on individual behavior and motivation. One of these is *xiao*, commonly translated as 'filial piety', understood as a child's virtue toward the parents — love and reverence for the parents, submission to their authority, financial support to aged parents, and bringing honor to the name of the family through tangible success (Kinney 1995b: 33; Tien 1997: 149). The other concept is *xue* 'learning', which is considered by Confucius as central to self-cultivation and the maintenance of social order (Schwartz 1985). Because in Chinese society excellence in learning continues to be a crucial means

---

4. However, the results did not replicate with a population from the University of California until ethnicity was controlled for as a confound due to the high proportion of Asian students on campus (Twenge 2008). According to Twenge, the ego inflation over generations can be partly attributed to the change in parenting and educational style in the last several decades characterized by the emphasis on self-esteem; the absence of a generational effect in narcissism scores among Asian students, on the other hand, can be attributed to the traditional collective values retained in the Asian American subculture.

of social mobility, much importance is placed on learning. The worship of learning in turn has given rise to the prioritization of academic success over other aspects of life (Chao & Tseng 2002). By tradition, filial piety and academic success are intimately related in the sense that they are mutually reinforcing. To the Chinese, one's own academic success is not so much a personal matter as a family honor and a symbol of love and respect for one's parents (Chao 1995, 1996). Filial piety demands academic achievements; doing well in school is taken directly as a manifestation of filial piety. Both practically serve to reinforce parental authority. Because parents are the culturally sanctioned authority over their children, and because academic success is highly valued in the culture, intense home-based parental involvement in children's learning is not only common (Ho 1995; Lau et al. 2011; Schneider & Lee 1990; Stevenson et al. 1993), but is also considered the primary responsibility of parents and a key criterion in judging the efficacy of parenting (Chao 1994; 1995; 1996; 2001). In this cultural context, parental authority, parental involvement, parental training (*jiaoxun*) and governance (*guan*) of the child are constitutive of the Confucian *li* 'rites' or "prescriptions of behavior" as the foundation of sociopolitical order (Schwartz 1985:71).

The prominence of filial piety and the high value of academic success have inevitably shaped the way childhood is viewed in the Chinese culture. Kinney (1995a: 12) observes that childhood is conceptualized as "a phase of human development which is not valued for its own merits", but for the potentials it holds for the future adult life. A child is considered incomplete but malleable, and childhood is dedicated to strict and intensive instruction for the prevention of deviant behavior and the building of virtues through the molding power of education. A natural part of the Confucian conceptualization of childhood is "a dim view of play and unrestrictive activities". This view of childhood, which, according to Kinney (1995b, 2003), was established as early as the Han dynasty (206 B.C.–220 A.D.), plays an enduring role in shaping the way adults treat children. The neo-Confucianism movement of the Song dynasty (960–1279 A.D.) renewed the tradition by emphasizing control, discipline, and punishment in the education of children (Bai 2005; Hsiung 2005). Throughout much of Chinese history, the conceptualization of childhood as a boot camp contributes to the perpetuation of a pedagogical approach geared toward academic achievements more than anything else. In light of the Chinese view of childhood, it comes as no surprise that the child's psychological wellbeing has not been a conventional concern in the culture (Eid & Diener 2001). As a result, the emotional consequences of negative control have never been seen as a problem and there is hardly any inhibitive force against the use of negativity.

Thus, taken together, institutionalized parental authority, culturally prescribed parental involvement, and a functionalist view of childhood give Chinese mothers higher-level justification of control over their children in hopes of preventing deviant behavior and driving them toward self-improvement and success. Seeing the maternal behavior as an effort to fulfill culturally prescribed parental role helps account for the pervasiveness and regularity of negative affective input in child-directed speech by Chinese mothers as social control strategies. Chinese mothers' affective verbal behavior shows that the mothers are highly assertive about their own authority and take for granted their children's submission. Their use of both anticipatory and reactive praise of obedience attests to the social cultural significance of parental authority in shaping maternal verbal behavior in interaction. In short, when Chinese mothers attempt to influence their children's performance by means of heightened control and negativity, their action is in line with the cultural priority of asserting parental authority and enforcing tangible success through authority.

Beside the major cultural differences in parenting, culture-specific socio-pragmatic conventions also influence patterns of maternal input. Specifically, the abundance of appreciative expressions such as *thank you* in the American data and the paucity of such expressions in the Chinese data reflect the socio-pragmatic norms governing verbal interaction in the two cultures. Gao and Ting-Toomey (1998:74) point out that thanking, just like apologizing, is "an integral part" of daily communication in the U.S., "used with everyone in every social and relational context". They attribute the emphasis on these politeness strategies to "the heightened concern for individual independence and autonomy" in American society where the fear of imposition runs deep. Grief and Gleason (1980) found that thanking is one of the earliest social routines explicitly taught to children in the U.S. Thus, from the perspective of socialization, the American mothers' expression of appreciation can be seen as a way of modeling a desirable politeness strategy. In contrast to Americans, as Gao and Ting-Toomey (1998:74) observe, the Chinese perceive the use of politeness markers including expressions of appreciation as socially distancing, especially inappropriate between family members and close friends. Cheng (2005:104) found that under identical conditions, native speakers of American English used thanking strategies more frequently than native speakers of Chinese, and their thanking strategies were more elaborate than those employed by their Chinese counterparts.[5] Cheng suggests that American egalitarianism and Chinese

---

5. These findings should not be taken as evidence that the Chinese never acknowledge favors received from others. Shih (1986) and Cheng (2005) converge in the finding that the Chinese tend to use a different strategy to acknowledge "indebtedness", namely apology, or an apologetic expression of embarrassment. The substitution of appreciation with apology has also been observed in the Japanese culture (Wierzbicka 2003), where a debt that is unpaid requires an apology (Cameron 2001). Gao and Ting-Toomey (1998:74) say that in close relationships where no verbal acknowledgment of favor is made, the Chinese expect that gratitude is "internalized and

hierarchy may be of relevance to the differential behaviors observed. To my mind, it is likely that multiple cultural factors interact in constraining how the Chinese use thanking strategies. But no matter what they are, it is clear that saying *thank you* is not a social strategy generally held in favor in the Chinese culture.

5.   Concluding remarks

In this study, I have shown that there are distinct cultural patterns in maternal affective input in American and Chinese mothers' child-directed speech. I have found a positivity bias in American maternal affective input characterized by praise and appreciation and low negativity. The opposite tendency, namely a negativity bias and low positivity, marks the Chinese mothers' affective communication. In addition, the two groups of mothers also differ more specifically in the types of positive and negative affective input they give their children. It is clear that Chinese and American children are exposed to very different affective speech acts and demeanor from an early age.

Given that this study is based on samples of a rather moderate size, the conclusions drawn here are not definitive. Further research is required with much larger samples, and with comparisons between mothers of children from different age groups, for broader generalizations about the cultural differences in maternal affective input. Also, since an effect of child gender on maternal praise has been documented (Koestner et al. 1989; Cantania 2009), it will be a future research goal to investigate how maternal affective input interacts with child gender across cultures. Furthermore, due to the multimodal nature of affective communication, future researchers will find it beneficial to include in their analysis systematic examinations of paralinguistic cues such as prosody, facial expressions, and body language. As noted in Section 2, the corpus data on which this study is based were collected almost twenty years ago. Yet in the last two decades China has undergone enormous socioeconomic change that transformed Chinese people's lives and lifestyle. One of the consequences of the change is an increased openness to Western lifestyles and modern approaches to parenting, especially among younger people. For this reason, the findings of this study might not reflect maternal behavioral tendencies typical of the younger generations with greater exposure to Western influence. The effect of such influence on parenting and maternal communicative style remains to be seen and future research is likely to benefit from generational or cross-temporal comparisons.

---

intuited". In general, it seems that the Chinese prefer implicit or indirect acknowledgments of indebtedness over open expressions of gratitude.

Notwithstanding the limitations, this study points to a cross-culturally significant linguistic phenomenon with ramifications beyond linguistics. On the one hand, the different patterns of the child-directed maternal affective communication cannot be fully understood without reference to the values, beliefs, socio-pragmatic conventions and practices that define cultural preoccupations. It seems that maternal verbal input as an important part of socialization is highly coherent with dominant cultural values, beliefs, and practices. On the other hand, because language is constitutive of cultural activities, different maternal affective verbal input will necessarily shape the process of socialization. Not only is socialization a mechanism by which children internalize cultural knowledge and ideology, and become recognized members of communities (Ochs 1996; Ochs and Schieffelin 2011). It is also a channel by which cultural norms are transmitted, instilled, and perpetuated (Clancy 1986; Keller and Greenfield 2000).

But my analysis raises more questions than it provides answers. First and foremost, focusing on maternal affective input as one side of the dyadic interaction, this study raises the question of whether distinct cultural patterns in maternal affective input correlate with distinct cultural patterns of child affective behavior on the production side of the dyadic story. Therefore, a cross-cultural perspective will benefit future research in child pragmatic development and shed light on child language development as part of socialization and acculturation.

Available cross-cultural comparative studies in parenting and parent–child interaction (e.g. Hess et al. 1987; Ng et al. 2007) focus on the effects of parental input on school performance across ethnic groups without looking at other important but more intangible aspects of human development such as emotional development. This study therefore raises further questions of (1) whether culture-specific maternal affective behavior, verbal and otherwise, may have different effects on the emotional development and psychological functioning of children, (2) to what extent academic success is enforced at the expense of child emotional wellbeing where school performance is overrated, and (3) what the differential psychological effects of culturally distinct parental strategies can tell us about childhood complexity and possibility that is beyond culture, Chinese or Western. This is an age where cultures constantly meet, mix, or collide, where cultural coherence can no longer be taken for granted, where "[w]e are becoming fluid and many-sided", to use the opening sentence of Lifton's (1999) book on *Human Resilience in an Age of Fragmentation*. Future cross-cultural research is required to explore the above questions, which have important implications for education, cross-cultural psychology, and inter-cultural communication in the age of cultural fluidity.

References

Azrin, N.H. & W.C, Holz. 1966. Punishment. *Operant behavior: areas of research and application*, ed. by W.K. Honig, 380–447. New York: Appleton-Century- Crofts.

Bai, Limin. 2005. *Shaping the Ideal Child: Children and Their Primers in Late Imperial China*. Hong Kong: The Chinese University Press.

Baker, Nancy D. & Keith E. Nelson. 1984. "Recasting and related conversational techniques for triggering syntactic advances by young children." *First Language* 5.3–21.

Bates, Elisabeth, Bretherton, Inge & Lynn S, Snyder. 1988. *From first words to grammar: Individual differences in dissociable mechanisms*. New York: Cambridge University Press.

Baumeister, Roy F., Campbell, Jennifer D., Krueger, Joachim I., Vohs, Kathleen D. 2003. "Does high self-esteem cause better performance, interpersonal success, happiness, or healthier lifestyles?" *Psychological Science in the Public Interest* 4:1.1–44.

Belsky, Jay. 1980. "Child maltreatment: An ecological integration." *American Psychologist* 35.320–335.

Belsky, Jay. 1984. "The determinants of parenting: A process model." *Child Development* 55.83–96.

Belsky, Jay, Lerner, Richard M. & Graham B, Spanier. 1984. *The Child in the Family*. Reading, MA: Addison-Wesley.

Bloom, Lois. 1993. *The Transition from Infancy to Language*. New York: Cambridge University Press.

Boccia, Maria & Joseph Campos. 1989. "Maternal emotional signals, social referencing, and infants' reactions to strangers." *New Directions for Child and Adolescent Development* 44. 25–49.

Bowlby, John. 1969. *Attachment*. New York: Basic Books.

Bowlby, John. 1976. *Separation: Anxiety and Anger*. New York: Basic Books.

Branden, Nathaniel. 1969. *The Psychology of Self-Esteem*. New York: Bantam.

Bronfenbrenner, Urie. 1977. "Toward an experimental ecology of human development." *American Psychologist* 32.513–531.

Calkins, Susan D., Smith, Cynthia L., Gill, Kathryn L. & Mary C, Johnson. 1998. "Maternal interactive style across contexts: Relations to emotional, behavioral, and physiological regulation during toddlerhood." *Social Development* 7.350–369.

Cameron, Deborah. 2001. *Working with Spoken Discourse*. London: Sage Publishing.

Cantania, Claire. 2009. *Praise, failure, and success: A corpus study*. University of Oregon honors thesis.

Chao, Ruth K. 1994. "Beyond parental control and authoritarian parenting style: Understanding Chinese parenting through the cultural notion of training." *Child Development* 65.1111–1119.

Chao, Ruth K. 1995. "Chinese and European-American cultural models of the self reflected in mothers' child-rearing beliefs." *Ethos* 23.328–354.

Chao, Ruth K. 1996. "Chinese and European American mothers' beliefs about the role of parenting in children's school success." *Journal of Cross-Cultural Psychology* 27.403–423.

Chao, Ruth K. 2001. "Extending research on the consequences of parenting style for Chinese Americans and European Americans." *Child Development* 72.1832–1843.

Chao, Ruth & Vivien, Tseng. 2002. "Parenting of Asians." *Handbook of Parenting: Vol. 4, Applied and Practical Parenting*, ed. by M.H. Bornstein. 59–93. Mahwah, NJ: Lawrence Erlbaum.

Cheng, Stephanie W. 2005. *An exploratory cross-sectional study of interlanguage pragmatic development of expressions of gratitude by Chinese learners of English*. Ph.D. dissertation, University of Iowa.

Cho, Grace E., Todd L. Sandel, Peggy J. Miller & Wang, Su-hua. 2005. "What do grandmothers think about self-esteem: American and Taiwanese folk theories revisited." *Social Development* 14:4.701–721.

Chua, Amy. 2011. *Battle Hymn of the Tiger Mother*. New York: Penguin Books.

Cimpian, A., Arce, H.M. C., Markman, E. M. & C. S, Dweck. 2007. "Subtle linguistic cues affect children's motivation." *Psychological Science* 18:4.314–316.

Clancy, Patricia M. 1986. "The Acquisition of Communicative style in Japanese." *Language Socialization across Cultures*, ed. by B. Schieffelin & E. Ochs, 213–250. Cambridge: University of Cambridge.

Cohn, Jeffrey F. & Edward Z, Tronick. 1983. "Three-month-old infants' reaction to simulated maternal depression." *Child Development* 54.185–193.

Duranti, Alessandro. 1997. *Linguistic Anthropology*. Cambridge: Cambridge University Press.

Duranti, Alessandro & Goodwin, Charles. ed. 1992. *Rethinking Context: Language as an Interactive Phenomenon*. Cambridge: Cambridge University Press.

Duranti, Alessandra, Ochs, Elinor & Schieffelin, Bambi (eds.). 2011. *The Handbook of Language Socialization*. Malden, MA: Blackwell.

Dweck, Carol S. 1999. "Caution: Praise can be dangerous." *American Educator* 23:1.4–9.

Dweck, Carol S. 2006. *Mindset*. New York: Random House.

Dweck, Carol S. 2007. "The Perils and Promises of Praise." *Educational Leadership* 65:2.34–39.

Eid, Michael & Diener, Ed. 2001. "Norms for Experiencing Emotions in Different Cultures: Inter- and intranational differences." *Journal of Personality and Social Psychology* 81.869–885.

Eisenberg, Ann R. 1986. "Teasing: Verbal play in two Mexicano homes." *Language Socialization across Cultures*, ed. by B. Schieffelin & E. Ochs, 182–198. Cambridge: Cambridge University Press.

Emde, Robert N., Kligman, David H., Reich, James H., & Ted D. Wade. 1978. "Emotional Expression in Infancy: I. Initial Studies of Social Signaling and an Emergent Model." *The Development of Affect*, ed. by M. Lewis & L.A. Rosenblum, 125–148. New York: Plenum.

Farrar, Michael J. 1990. "Discourse and the Acquisition of Grammatical Morphemes." *Journal of Child Language* 17.607–624.

Gao, Ge & Ting-Toomey, Stella. 1998. *Communicating Effectively with the Chinese*. London: Sage Publications.

Gelman, Susan A. & Gail D, Heyman. 1999. "Carrot-eaters and creature-believers: The Effects of Lexicalization on Children's Inferences about social Categories." *Psychological Science* 10:6.489–493.

Grief, Esther B. & Jean B, Gleason. 1980. "Hi, thanks, and goodbye: More routine information." *Language in Society* 9:2.156–166.

Gumperz, John & Dell, Hymes. ed. 1972. *Directions in Sociolinguistics: The Ethnography of Communication*. New York. Holt, Rinehart and Winston.

Hampson, June & Nelson, Katherine. 1993. "The Relation of Maternal Language to Variation in Rate and Style of Language Acquisition." *Journal of Child Language* 20.313–342.

Heine, Steven J. 2005. "Where is the evidence for pancultural self-enhancement? A reply to Sedikides, Gaertner, and Toguchi (2003)." *Journal of Personality and Social Psychology* 89.531–538.

Heine, Steven J. & Takeshi, Hamamura. 2007. "In search of East Asian self-enhancement." *Personality and Social Psychology Review* 11.4–27.

Heine, Steven J., Kitayama, Shinobu, & Darrin R, Lehman. 2001. "Cultural differences in self-evaluation: Japanese readily accept negative self-relevant information." *Journal of Cultural Psychology* 32.434–443.

Heine, Steven J., Lehman, Darrin R., Markus, Hazel R., & Shinobu, Kitayama. 1999. "Is there a universal need for positive self-regard?" *Psychological Review* 106.766–794.

Hess, Robert D., Chang, Chih-Mei, & Teresa M, McDevitt. 1987. Cultural variations in family beliefs about children's performance in mathematics: Comparisons among People's Republic of China, Chinese-American, and Caucasian-American families." *Journal of Educational Psychology* 79.179–188.

Hinde, Robert A. 1979. *Toward Understanding Relationships*. London: Academic Press.

Hinde, Robert A. & Stevenson-Hinde, Joan. 1987. "Interpersonal relationships and child development." *Developmental Review* 7.1–21.

Ho, Esther Sui-chu. 1995. "Parent Involvement: A comparison of different definitions and explanations." *Education Journal* 23.39–68.

Hsiung, Ping-Chen. 2005. *A Tender Voyage: Children and Childhood in Late Imperial China*. Stanford, CA: Stanford University Press.

Hymes, Dell. 1964. *Language in Culture and Society*. New York: Harper and Row.

Jing-Schmidt, Zhuo. 2009. "Positivity and negativity in early mother–child communication: Data from three cultures." Paper presented on the 17th Annual Meeting: Symposium about Language and Society, April, Austin, Texas, 2009.

Kamins, Melissa L. and Dweck, Carol S. 1999. Person versus process praise and criticism: Implications for contingent self-worth and coping. *Developmental Psychology* 35(3), 835–847.

Keller, Heidi & Patricia M. Greenfield. 2000. "History and Future Development in Cross-Cultural Psychology." *Journal of Cross-Cultural Psychology* 31.52–62.

Kinney, Anne B. 1995a. "Introduction." *Chinese Views of Childhood*, ed. by A. B. Kinney, 11–16. Honolulu, HI: University of Hawaii Press.

Kinney, Anne B. 1995b. "Dyed silk: Han Notions of the Moral Development of Children." *Chinese Views of Childhood*, ed. by A.B. Kinney, 17–56. Honolulu, HI: University of Hawaii Press.

Kinney, Anne B. 2003. *Representations of Childhood and Youth in Early China*. Stanford, CA: Stanford University Press.

Klinnert, M. 1984. "The regulation of infant behavior by maternal facial expression." *Infant Behavior and Development* 7.447–465.

Koestner, Richard, Zuckerman, Miron, & Julia, Koestner. 1989. "Attributional focus of praise and children's intrinsic motivation: The moderating role of gender." *Personality and Social Psychology Bulletin* 15.61–72.

Kohn, Alfie. 2001. "Five reasons to stop saying, 'good job!'" *Young Children* 56:5.24–30.

Lagacé Séguin, Daniel G. & Robert J. Coplan. 2005. "Maternal Emotional Styles and Child Social Adjustment: Assessment, Correlates, Outcomes and Goodness of fit in early Childhood." *Social Development* 14:4.613–636.

Langacker, R., 1987. *Foundations of Cognitive Grammar, Vol.1, Theoretical Prerequisites*. Stanford University Press, Stanford

Lau, Eva Y.H., Li, Hui & Nirmala, Rao. 2011. "Parental Involvement and Children's readiness for school in China." *Educational Research* 53:1.95–113.

Levy, Robert I. 1984. "Emotion, knowing, and culture." *Culture Theory*, ed. by R. Shweder & R. LeVine, 214–237. Cambridge: Cambridge University Press.

Lifton, Robert J. 1999. *The Protean Self: Human Resilience in an Age of Fragmentation*. Chicago: University of Chicago Press.

Lo, Adrienne & Heidi, Fung. 2011. "Language socialization and shaming." *The Handbook of Language Socialization*, ed. by A. Duranti, E. Ochs & B. Schieffelin, 169–189. Malden, MA: Wiley-Blackwell.

MacWhinney, Brian. 1991. *The CHILDES project: Tools for analyzing talk*. Hillsdale, NJ: Lawrence Erlbaum.

Main, Mary, Tomosini, Lisa & William, Tolan. 1979. "Differences among Mothers of Infants judged to Differ in Security." *Developmental Psychology* 15:4.472–273.

Markus, Hazel R. & Shinobu, Kitayama. 1991. "Culture and self: Implications for Cognition, Emotion, and Motivation." *Psychological Review* 98.224–253.

Markus, Hazel R. & Shinobu, Kitayama. 1994. "The Cultural Construction of Self and Emotion: Implications for Social Behavior." *Emotion and Culture: Empirical Studies of Mutual Influence*, ed. by H.R. Markus & S. Kitayama, 89–130. Washington, DC: American Psychological Association.

Maslow, Abraham H. 1943. "A Theory of Human Motivation." *Psychological Review* 50.370–396.

Maslow, Abraham H. 1954. *Motivation and Personality*. New York: Harper and Row.

Mikulincer, Mario, Phillip R. Shaver & Pereg, Dana. 2003. "Attachment theory and affect regulation: The dynamics, development, and cognitive consequences of attachment-related strategies." *Motivation and Emotion* 27:2.77–102.

Miller Peggy J. 1986. "Teasing as Language Socialization and Verbal Play in A White Working-Class Community." *Language Socialization across Cultures*, ed. by B. Schieffelin & E. Ochs, 199–212. Cambridge: Cambridge University Press.

Miller, Peggy J., Wiley, Angela R. Fung, Heidi & Liang, Chung-Hui. 1997. "Personal storytelling as a medium of socialization in Chinese and American families." *Child Development* 68.557–568.

Miller, Peggy J., Wang, Su-hua, Sandel, Todd, & Grace E, Cho. 2002. "Self-esteem as folk theory: A comparison of European American and Taiwanese mothers' beliefs." *Parenting: Science and Practice* 2.209–239.

Murray, Ann D., Jeanne Johnson & Jo Peters. 1990. "Fine-tuning of utterance length to Preverbal Infants: Effects on Later Language Development." *Journal of Child Language* 17.511–525.

Ng, Florrie F.-Y., Pomerantz, Eva, & Lam, Shuo-fong. 2007. "European American and Chinese parents responses to children's success and failure: Implications for children's responses." *Developmental Psychology* 43:5.1239–1255.

Ochs, Elinor. 1986. "Introduction." *Language Socialization across Culture*, ed. by B. Schieffelin & E. Ochs, 1–16. Cambridge: University of Cambridge Press.

Ochs, Elinor. 1988. *Culture and language development: Language acquisition and language socialization in a Samoan village*. Cambridge: Cambridge University Press.

Ochs, Elinor, ed. 1989. "The Pragmatics of Affect." Special issue of *Text* 9:1.93–124.

Ochs, Elinor. 1996. "Linguistic Resources for Socializing Humanity." *Rethinking Linguistic Relativity*, ed. by J. J. Gumperz and S. C. Levinson, 407–437. Cambridge: Cambridge University Press.

Ochs, Elinor & Schieffelin, Bambi. 2011. "The theory of Language Socialization." *The Handbook of Language Socialization*, ed. by A. Duranti, E. Ochs & B. Schieffelin, 1–21. Malden, MA: Wiley-Blackwell.

Odom, Samuel L., & Strain, Philip S. 2002. "Evidence based practice in early intervention: early childhood special education." *Single subject design research. Journal of Early Intervention* 25.151–160.

Patterson, Gerald R. 1982. *Coercive Family Process*. Eugene, OR: Castalia.

Rosaldo, Renato. 1980. *Ilongot Headhunting*. Stanford: Stanford University Press.

Schieffelin, Bambi. 1986. "Teasing and shaming in Kaluli children's interactions." *Language Socialization across Cultures*, ed. by B. Schieffelin & E. Ochs, 165–181. Cambridge: Cambridge University Press.

Schieffelin, Bambi & Ochs, Elinor, eds, 1986. *Language Socialization across Cultures*. Cambridge: Cambridge University Press.

Schneider, Barbara & Lee, Yongsook 1990. "A model for academic success: The school and home environment of East Asian students." *Anthropology and Education Quarterly* 21:4.358–377.

Schwartz, Benjamin I. 1985. *The World of Thought in Ancient China*. Cambridge, MA: the Belknap Press of Harvard University Press.

Shih, Yu-hwei. E. 1986. *Conversational Politeness and Foreign Language Teaching*. Taipei, Taiwan: Crane Publishing.

Shore, Allan. 1994. *Affect Regulation and the Origin of the Self*. NJ: Lawrence Erlbaum.

Skinner, Burrhus F. 1970. *Walden Two*. Toronto: Macmillan.

Sorce, James F., & Emde, Robert N. 1981. "Mother's presence is not enough: Effect of emotional availability on infant exploration." *Developmental Psychology* 17.737-745.

Strain, Philip, Kerr, Mary M., Stagg, Vaughan, Lambert, Donna, & Lenkner, Deborah. 1984. "An empirical definition of elementary school adjustment." *Behavior Modification* 8.51–473.

Strain, Philip & Kohler, Frank W.1998. "Expanding peer-mediated interventions." *Topics in Early Childhood Special Education* 18.48–60.

Stevenson, H.W., Chen, C. & S.-Y, Lee. 1993. "Mathematics achievement of Chinese, Japanese, and American children: Ten years later." *Science* 259.53–58.

Tardif, Twila, Gelman, Susan A., & Xu, Fan. 1999. "Putting the 'noun bias' in context: A comparison of English and Mandarin." *Child Development* 70:3.620–635.

Taylor, Nicole, Wilberta Donovan, Sally Miles & Leavitt, Lewis. 2009. "Maternal Control strategies, maternal language usage and children's language usage at two years." *Journal Child Language* 36.381–404.

Tien, Ju-Kang. 1997. *Male Anxiety and Female Chastity: A Comparative Study of Chinese Ethical Values in Ming-Ching Times*. Boston, M.A.: Brill Academic Publication.

Tomasello, Michael & Jody Todd. 1983. "Joint Attention and Lexical Acquisition Style." *First Language* 4.197–212.

Twenge, Jean M. 2006. *Generation Me: Why Today's Young Americans are More Confident, Assertive, Entitled… and More Miserable Than Ever Before*. New York: Free Press.

Twenge, Jean M. & W. Keith Campbell. 2001. "Age and birth cohort differences in self-esteem: A cross-temporal meta-analysis." *Personality and Social Psychology Review* 5.321–344.

Twenge, Jean. M., Konrath, Sara, Foster, Joshua D., Campbell, W. Keith & Brad J, Bushman. 2008a. "Egos inflating over time: A cross-temporal meta-analysis of the Narcissistic Personality Inventory." *Journal of Personality* 76.875–901.

Twenge, Jean. M., Konrath, Sara, Foster, Joshua D., Campbell, W. Keith & Brad J, Bushman. 2008b. "Further Evidence of an Increase in Narcissism Among college Students." *Journal of Personality* 76.919–927.

Twenge, Jean M. 2008. "Generation Me, the origins of birth cohort Differences in Personality Traits, and Cross-Temporal Meta-Analysis." *Social and Personality Psychology Compass* 2:3.1440–1454.

Volling, Brenda L., McElwain, Nancy L. & Alison L, Miller. 2002. "Emotion regulation in context: The Jealousy Complex Between Young Siblings and its Relation with Child and Family characteristics." *Child Development* 73.581–600.

Webster-Stratton, C. 1999. *How to promote children's social and emotional competence.* London: Paul Chapman.

Wierzbicka, Anna. 1994. "Emotion, Language, and Cultural scripts." *Emotion and Culture: Empirical Studies of Mutual Influence,* ed. by H.R. Markus & S. Kitayama, 133–196. Washington, DC: American Psychological Association.

Wierzbicka, Anna. 1999. *Emotions across Languages and Cultures: Diversity and Universals.* Cambridge: Cambridge University Press.

Wierzbicka, Anna. 2003. *Cross-cultural Pragmatics: The Semantics of Human Interaction.* Berlin/New York: Mouton De Gruyter.

Wolery, M. 2000. "Recommended practices in child-focused interventions" *DEC Recommended Practices,* ed. by S. Sandall, M. E.McLean, & B. J. Smith, 34–38. Longmont, CO: Sopris West.

Zhou, Jing & Jin, Lixian. 2012. "Do educational backgrounds make a difference? A comparative study on communicative acts of Chinese mothers in interacting with their young children." *Chinese Language and Discourse* 3:1.90–109. Special Issue on *Development of Pragmatic and Discourse skills in Chinese-Speaking Children,* ed. by Z. Hua & L. Jin reprinted in this volume.

Do educational backgrounds make a difference?

A comparative study on communicative acts of Chinese mothers in interacting with their young children

Jing Zhou and Lixian Jin
East China Normal University / De Montfort University

For decades there has been a debate about whether parents with different socioeconomic status have differential influences on their children's language development. This study focuses on the features of language use of Mandarin-speaking mothers with different educational backgrounds in interaction with their 3–6 year old children to explore the similarities and differences between the mothers' communication with their children. Data were collected from videotaped semi-structured mother–child interactions among different age groups. The main research finding reveals that the communicative acts of these Chinese mothers are similar at the levels of social interchange and the speech act; the common types of communicative acts show a cultural consistency among Chinese mothers in interacting with their young children. However, the language inputs of mothers of the two differing social groups show significant differences on linguistic productivity, vocabulary measurement and pragmatic flexibility. These findings are discussed in the context of the role of mothers' input in language development.

1. Introduction

The sociologist Bernstein (1971, 1973) claimed in a long series of research papers that the social and cultural differences of parents may have an impact on their children's language development and, consequently, on some children's progress at school. Within the context of his sociolinguistic theory of socialization, Bernstein's theory held that there were different abstract 'codes' underlying the speech used to children and that these codes were deeply associated with different social classes; the codes were said to negatively influence some children in their education since schools demand a particular code which might not be used at home. This sociologically-oriented theory of language codes had a wide impact on education in the 1970s-1990s; it was taught to several generations of teachers during their training as an explanation for the school failure of working class children. Since then, there has been continuous concern about whether differentiated language of parents addressed to children, particularly the speech of mothers from lower socio-economic classes, might limit their children's language development (MacWhinney & Osser 1977; Hart & Risley 1995; Hammer &Weiss 1999). Bernstein (1971, 1973) argued that mothers from middle-class backgrounds use an 'elaborated code' of language to communicate with their children while mothers from lower-class backgrounds tend to use a 'restricted code' with their children. According to Bernstein (ibid.), the 'elaborated code' contains features of more abstractive, analytical and explicit expressions and this code is favoured by schools; however, the 'restricted code' lacks such features, but stresses social solidarity through the use of inexplicit and less referenced expressions. Bernstein's theories were given a prominent place in much 'standard' literature in sociolinguistics (e.g. Trudgill 1974; Dittmar 1976; Halliday 1978, Fasold 1990; Wardhaugh 1992), social psychology (e.g. Giles & Powesland 1975), language acquisition (e.g. de Villiers and de Villiers 1978; Romaine 1984; Anderson 1990) and language education (e.g. Trudgill 1975; Stubbs 1986). At the same time, they were often vigorously critiqued because it was alleged that they led to a 'deficit' assumption in that children from lower social classes had limited language because of the codes which in effect delayed their school progress (Edwards 1976; Edwards 1979; Gordon 1981). While this misunderstanding was largely a mis-reading of both language development and of Bernstein's work (Atkinson 1985; Bernstein 1994), it led to much research in Europe and Australia to investigate social class 'difference' as simply a difference of codes which are potentially valid for different situations rather than the 'deficit' position, which implied educational inadequacy and linguistic inferiority of the working class codes (Robinson 1978).

Further research has been carried out, following the argument of Bernstein's sociolinguistic theories of socialization on child language development. MacWhinney and Osser (1977) gathered data from 20 British 5-year-old children to focus on hesitation phenomena in order to examine the verbal planning functions of children's speech. Their research showed 'there was no significant main effect for social class and only a weak interaction of sex with social class' (ibid p.978). Researchers have also paid attention to the interaction between mother and child from a pragmatic viewpoint to investigate precisely how the process of such interaction might influence child language development. They have particularly examined mothers' educational backgrounds in relation to the language development of their children. Hart and Risley (1995) carried out an investigation to collect monthly samples of parent–child interaction data from 42 families of three types: professional, working-class and welfare-receiving families over a 36 month period. Their results show that 3 year-old children from professional families have larger vocabulary inventories compared with those of children from welfare-receiving families; within a year, children from professional families heard around 11 million words in verbal interaction, compared to children from welfare-receiving families who merely heard about 3 million words. Also, the middle-class parents tended to offer choices to their children during interaction, rather than giving direct behavioural instructions, which occurred among parents from welfare-receiving families (Hart & Risley 1995). Furthermore, findings from other research projects (Hammer & Weiss 1999; Hoff et al. 2002; Hoff & Naigles 2002; Hoff & Tian 2005) demonstrate that there is a difference of adult–child interaction patterns between mothers who have a higher educational background (HEB) and social-economic position and those who have a lower educational background (LEB) and social-economic position. The former tend to provide more interactive opportunities to their children using a wider range of vocabulary and questions. The latter appear to interact less with their children, use a narrower range of vocabulary and ask fewer questions; instead, they give more instructions. Based on this evidence, these researchers (ibid.) argue that mothers' educational background has an important role in child language development regarding frequency of interaction, richness of vocabulary, asking questions and mean length of utterances.

While research on the differential influences of mothers' language use towards child language development has been developing in the West since the 1970s, there is little published research regarding how the language use of Chinese parents influences their children's language development. In particular, very few studies investigate the language features of Mandarin-speaking mothers in interaction with their children (cf. Jing-Schmidt, this volume; Huang 2011).

This chapter aims to report on a project which investigates the following research questions:

– How do mothers and children interact in a Chinese context?
– Are there any differences between mothers with different educational backgrounds which have an impact on child language use in interaction?
– Do Chinese mothers' language use and interactive patterns influence child language use and their interaction development?

2. Method

2.1 Participants

This study explores the language use of communicative acts in two groups of Mandarin-speaking mothers as they interacted with their children who were at the age intervals of 36, 42, 48, 54, 60, 66 and 72 months. Each group had 20 pairs of mothers and children. One group includes mothers from middle class families. They have a higher educational background (abbreviated as HEB) and are professionals: government officers, editors, teachers, accountants or technicians in companies. The other group of mothers had lower educational backgrounds (LEB) and worked in factories or companies as workers. Among this second group, the highest educational level was in a technical vocational school. Both groups of mothers use Mandarin as the communicative language to talk with their children at home. All the children in the different age groups are the only child of their family and all were identified by their teachers as normal in language development.

2.2 Procedure

The data collection followed the procedure presented below for both groups of mothers interacting with their children. Mother–child pairs were brought to a normal kindergarten classroom. The interaction between each mother and her child was videotaped using a camcorder located at one corner of the room operated by remote control. For each session, there was a warm-up period at the beginning, during which the mothers and children had a free play session with the collection of toys in the room and the mother was instructed to take a few minutes to let her child become accustomed to the setting. After this warm-up period, there was a period of semi-structured play in which each mother played with her child using the contents of four boxes. The four boxes contained:

a. a ball for initiating the face-to-face interaction between mother and child; each mother and child could roll or throw the ball to each other, or talk about the ball;
b. a popular toy (a 'Transformer') to encourage the child and mother to talk and play together with this manipulative toy;
c. paper and crayons for mother and child to draw pictures and talk about them; and
d. a picture book with stories in Chinese, for each mother to initiate communication about reading with the child by looking at, talking about and discussing pictures, texts and related topics.

There was no specific instruction to parents regarding how many minutes should be spent with each box, but they were asked to have only one box open at a time (and thus focus on one at a time), and to try to do some activities with all four boxes in about 10 minutes. The mother was told that the session would be terminated if she tried to engage the child in all four activities at the same time. Each videotaped session lasted for about 20 minutes, including a warm-up, main activities and finishing-off.

2.3 Data analysis

The data from the videotapes were transcribed, transferred into computer files, and formatted in accordance with the *Codes for the Human Analysis of Transcripts (CHAT)* (MacWhinney 1991) using the transcription conventions for analysis by the CLAN software available through the *Child Language Data Exchange System* (CHILDES; MacWhinney & Snow 1985, 1990; MacWhinney 1991). Transcripts were verified between a first and a second transcriber, both for content and for adherence to the transcription conventions required by CHAT. Utterance boundaries were based first on contour and secondly on pause duration. Using the Inventory of Communicative Acts (INCA-A), parent–child interaction was first segmented into communicative acts, each of which could be assigned one code on each of two levels: (a) the level of social interchange; and (b) the specific speech act. A full listing of INCA codes used is provided in Ninio et al. (1990). Inter-rater reliability was estimated separately for the pragmatic measurement of social interchange and speech act codes. Reliability between two coders was calculated at 90% for interchange codes, and 85% for speech act codes. This offers a reasonably high reliability for the analysis of the transcribed and coded utterances in this project.

3. Results

3.1 Comparison of the mothers' communicative participation

One of the key aspects that this project has looked into is participation through the frequency of utterance in the parent–child interaction. This is a topic which has received attention in studies of parental–child interaction and pragmatics (e.g. Ninio & Snow 1996; Mahoney et al. 1998; Zhou 2002; Desforges 2003). In this study, the participation frequency (i.e. the total number of utterances per minute) in mother–child interaction has been examined with regard to the different educational backgrounds. the findings show that mothers with HEB participated more than those with LEB.

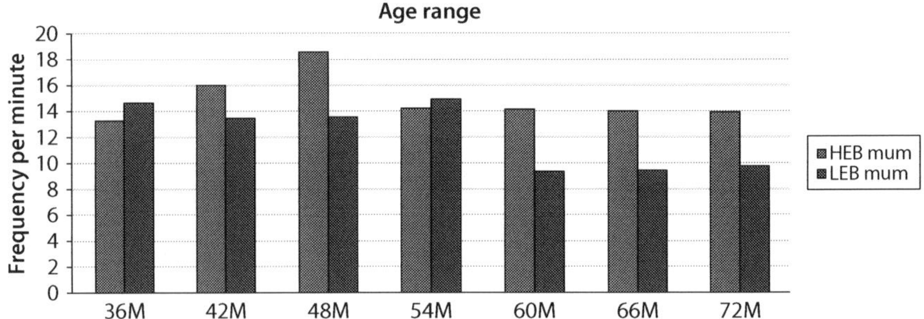

Figure 1. The average frequency of participation in mother–child interactions by mothers with different educational backgrounds

With reference to age (see Figure 1), as the age of the children increases up to 48 months, the participation frequency increases with mothers of HEB and in fact overall there is a statistical difference ($F_{(1,139)} = 4.093$, $p < 0.05$) in participation frequency between the two groups of mothers. This outcome indicates that the language input from mothers with HEB is more frequent than that given by mothers with LEB and that this seems more consistently so as children's age increases.

3.2 Comparison of mothers' communicative interchanges

In the Inventory of Communicative Acts-Abridge (INCA-A; Ninio et al. 1990), three levels of the communicative interchanges have been included: social interchanges, speech acts and pragmatic flexibility. These categories are used to explore the features of social interactive functions, expression and fluency that participants have for every speech act of their interaction. Social interchanges are used to examine how participants negotiate their mutual intentions towards each other in interactions; they are sub-categorized into 22 types of codes, including discussion, negotiation, marking and meta-communication. The investigation of speech acts in this study included analysing which methods the speakers used to express interactive intentions with 65 coding types, such as directives/comments and answers, speech inducements and answers, promises and answers, announcements and answers, statements and answers, questions and answers. The combination of social interchanges and speech acts creates the levels of pragmatic flexibility. It is observed that social interchanges and speech acts represent the fundamental pragmatic competence of a speaker while the capability of speech negotiation of speakers shows their competence of pragmatic flexibility. Some previous research has been conducted in different languages using this system of analysis (Ninio & Snow 1996; Zhou 2002; Hiromi 2002; Keşli 2006).

3.2.1 *Social interchanges by mothers with different educational backgrounds in interactions with their children*

Social interchange is an essential element for individuals to express their social intentions in interactions with others over a number of turns within the same topic. This interaction provides the contextualised social exchanges. Two aspects of social interchanges which have been looked into in this chapter are the average usage of social interchanges per session between mothers and children of different age groups and frequency of different types of social interchanges used by mothers of different educational backgrounds. The average usage presents a general picture of the social interchanges between mothers and children of different ages and the frequency shows the intensity of chosen types of social interchanges the mothers used with children of different age groups.

The findings indicate that the average usage of types of social interchanges is similar for mothers of different educational backgrounds: there is no statistical difference ($F_{(1,139)} = 1.133$, $p = .289 > .05$). Mothers with different educational backgrounds tend to use four types of social interchanges (see Table. 1) frequently and consistently as children's age increases. They are Discussing Joint Focus (DJF), Negotiating Immediate Activity (NIA), Discussing Hearer's Attention (DHA) and Discussing Clarification of Action (DCA). These four types of social interchanges together account for 70% of the usage in relation to all social interchange types among these mothers of different educational backgrounds with children aged 3–6 years. This strongly suggests that Chinese mothers mainly use these four types of social interchanges for their interaction with children.

However, further examination of the data shows some differentiation in frequency of use of social interchanges between HEB and LEB mothers with different age groups of children. It is interesting to see (Figure 2) that HEB mothers tend to use the four types with a high frequency with children aged 3. Yet, as the age of children increases, this frequency is decreased. The data suggest that mothers with HEB expand the use of social interchange types from the focused four to other types more readily than mothers with LEB. This indicates that mothers with HEB may make greater effort to follow the needs and demands of their children's development, gradually reduce their control and directives in interaction, and increase other types of social interchanges with their children, e.g. showing attention to hearer, reading written text, etc. This tendency also appears in the examination of their speech acts (see Figure 3), which is discussed next.

Table 1. Comparison of the mean proportion of the core Social Interchange types at each age: HEB mothers and LEB mothers (%)

Social interchange types	Age Range													
	36M		42M		48M		54M		60M		66M		72M	
	H	L	H	L	H	L	H	L	H	L	H	L	H	L
DJF: Discussing Joint Focus	37.6	35.0	35.1	36.0	35.1	39.4	37.2	39.0	38.1	40.8	40.6	41.2	36.2	43.6
NIA: Negotiating Immediate Activity	32.5	28.7	30.9	31.9	34.4	26.4	30.28	31.5	26.6	26.4	24.0	17.3	23.0	26.6
DHA: Directing Hearer's Attention	7.8	8.7	6.4	10.0	5.0	6.5	4.1	6.9	7.3	9.9	3.2	4.7	4.3	4.6
DCC: Discussing clarification of verbal communication	5.3	7.3	5.0	4.9	3.8	6.3	3.9	3.5	4.1	4.5	4.3	8.0	6.1	5.1
DCA: Discussing Clarification of Action	2.1	5.5	4.3	3.7	6.3	2.6	4.5	5.5	2.2	1.5	3.5	4.3	3.2	3.8
MRK: Marking	2.0	2.5	1.0	1.6	1.7	1.9	1.1	1.2	1.6	1.9	1.3	2.7	1.7	.92
DRE: Discussing Recent Event	1.7	1.5	1.9	1.6	3.2	1.6	2.7	2.1	2.5	1.6	2.9	2.0	3.0	2.5
DRP: Discussing the Related-to- present	1.7	2.6	2.7	2.8	2.1	4.6	2.9	2.9	2.9	1.9	2.6	2.2	4.7	1.5
TXT: Reading Written Text	1.2	2.4	7.2	6.1	4.0	6.1	8.3	7.9	9.5	7.6	13.6	11.4	9.5	6.6
SAT: Show attention to hearer	/	/	1.4	1.2	1.2	1.8	1.6	/	1.9	1.5	1.9	1.4	2.3	1.5
DFW: Discussing Fantasy World	5.0	2.2	4.5	1.0	1.1	1.5	/	/	/	/	/	/	/	1.5
DNP: Discussing Non-present	/	/	/	/	/	/	/	1.9	/	1.1	.34	3.0	1.5	/
DHS: Discussing Hearer's Thoughts and Feelings	/	/	/	1.0	/	/	/	/	/	/	/	/	1.5	/

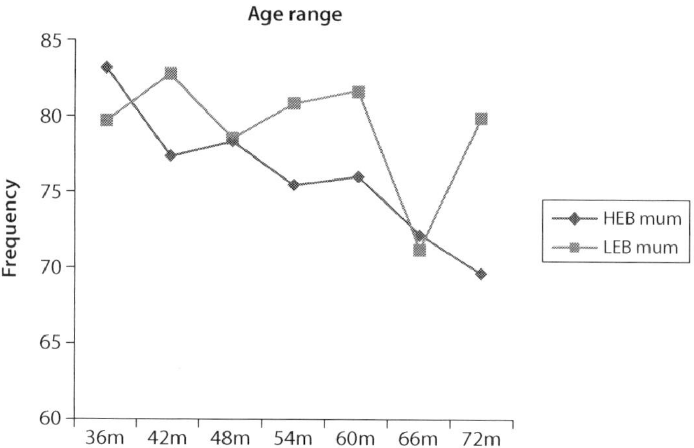

Figure 2. Frequency of 4 types of social interchanges used by mothers with different educational backgrounds with children aged 3–6

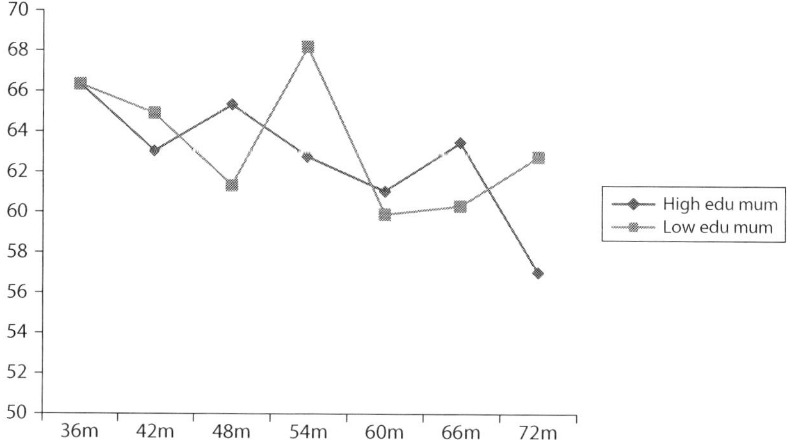

Figure 3. Frequency of 4 types of speech acts used by mothers with different educational backgrounds with children aged 3–6

3.2.2   *Comparison of speech acts of mothers with different educational backgrounds*

The types of speech acts used by these mothers with different educational backgrounds are examined through investigating 22 speech acts in the data (Figure 3). The findings show that overall there is no statistical significance ($F_{(1,139)} = .595$, $p = .442 > .05$) in speech acts between the two groups of Chinese mothers interacting with their children between 3 and 6 years.

Table 2 presents the frequency of these 22 types of speech acts used by these mothers with their children. It indicates similarity in the average usage and frequency

Table 2. Frequency of Speech Act types used by mothers in different age groups (%)

Speech act types	Age groups													
	36M		42M		48M		54M		60M		66M		72M	
	H	L	H	L	H	L	H	L	H	L	H	L	H	L
RP: Request/proposes	23.6	21.5	23.1	23.5	24.0	18.1	20.8	25.3	21.2	22.1	19.1	13.0	16.2	22.2
ST: State or make a declarative statement	12.1	16.3	13.0	14.4	17.7	14.1	18.1	18.4	16.1	16.0	18.2	17.1	14.4	19.0
QN: Ask a product-question (Wh-question)	18.0	14.1	15.7	14.3	13.9	15.3	10.9	12.6	14.4	11.1	14.1	18.6	13.8	12.2
YQ: Ask a yes-no-question	12.7	14.6	11.3	12.8	9.8	13.9	13.0	12.0	9.4	10.8	12.2	11.7	12.7	9.5
SA: Answer a Wh-question by statement	2.9	2.1	3.0	2.9	1.6	2.5	2.8	3.3	2.6	2.5	3.5	4.8	3.2	4.2
GR: Give reasons	2.4	2.0	1.7	1.8	1.3	1.1	.98	1.6	3.1	1.9	1.3	.61	1.4	1.1
MK: Mark occurrence of event	2.3	.70	2.0	2.6	1.9	1.5	1.5	1.2	2.8	3.8	2.2	2.9	1.6	1.1
RT: Repeat/imitate other's utterance	2.1	3.4	2.9	2.9	2.0	3.3	2.4	1.6	1.9	1.4	2.5	4.4	3.1	3.0
TX: Read or recite written text aloud	.46	1.6	4.6	2.8	2.6	5.0	6.5	4.9	7.9	5.3	9.2	6.9	6.7	3.5
AB: Approve of appropriate behavior.	2.0	1.7	2.4	1.1	3.2	.48	3.0	2.4	1.7	2.5	1.2	2.3	1.0	1.4
EQ: Eliciting question	2.5	1.4	1.9	2.0	2.4	3.0	2.1	2.4	2.4	2.3	2.4	2.6	2.5	2.3
SI: State intent to carry out act by speaker	1.7	2.3	1.4	2.4	1.4	2.2	1.0	2.0	1.5	2.0	1.6	.72	1.4	1.0
AC: Show attentiveness to communications.	1.4	1.7	1.4	2.7	2.1	4.3	3.4	2.3	2.2	1.9	2.9	2.1	4.3	6.3
AP: Agree with proposition	1.9	1.5	1.8	2.2	2.1	1.9	2.3	1.7	2.3	2.3	1.8	1.6	1.1	.58
AQ: Aggravated question, expression of disapproval by restating a question.	1.7	.91	1.2	.50	.71	1.0	.44	.81	1.2	2.4	.60	.72	1.4	1.4
CR: Criticize or point out error in nonverbal behavior.	.31	.10	.10	.15	0	.22	.10	.81	.45	.83	1.2	.94	1.2	.95
CS: Counter-suggestion; an indirect refusal.	.31	.28	.26	.34	.19	.29	.36	.49	.71	.11	.48	.28	.33	.21
CT: Correct, provide correct verbal form in place of erroneous one.	.66	.52	.23	.38	.19	.41	.77	.28	.63	.22	.36	.67	.63	.84
DS: Disapprove, scold, and protest disruptive behavior.	.46	.80	.65	.69	.82	.35	.58	.42	.56	.66	.30	.17	.52	.95
ET: Exclaim in surprise or enthusiasm	.58	2.1	.91	1.1	1.6	1.4	1.4	1.5	.52	1.3	.42	1.5	2.2	1.4
PM: Praise for motor acts	.46	.52	.94	.34	2.3	.54	1.5	.92	.30	.77	.42	.55	1.6	.53
RQ: Yes/no question which functions as a suggestion	3.4	3.6	3.4	2.4	2.2	3.1	2.3	.95	1.5	1.6	.78	1.4	.82	.53

of speech act types by these mothers. Further, as in the social interchanges, these Chinese mothers with different educational backgrounds tend to use 4 types of speech acts with a high frequency. They are: Request/proposes (RP), State or make a declarative statement (ST), Ask for a product-question, i.e. Wh-Question (QN) and Ask a yes-no question (YQ). Regardless of their educational backgrounds, these 4 types amount to over 60% of the total number of speech acts in their interaction with children, shown in Table 2 regarding the frequency of speech act types used. This phenomenon may be interpreted as showing that Chinese mothers choose or like to use the four types of RP, ST, QN and YQ rather than other speech act types in their interaction with children. Some speech acts, such as Give reasons (GR), Criticise or point out errors in nonverbal behaviour (CR), Counter-suggestion, indirect refusals (CS), Praise for motor acts (PM), etc. have low frequency.

3.2.3   *Levels of Pragmatic flexibility by mothers with different backgrounds in interaction with children*

Pragmatic flexibility represents the ability to use different speech acts to achieve the same social interchanges or to use the same speech act with different social interchanges. It is calculated here by examining the frequency of combinations of Social Interchanges (using the codes shown in Table 1) and Speech Acts (using the codes shown in Table 2): the wider the range of types of pragmatic flexibility which are used, the more this shows the language users are able to express themselves in a flexible way. Unlike the other two aspects (social interchanges and speech acts, in which mothers with different educational backgrounds have a similar use of the main four types in each aspect, (see Tables 1 and 2) some statistically significant differences ($F_{(1,139)} = 4.039$, $p < 0.05$) are found in terms of pragmatic flexibility between mothers with different educational backgrounds (see Table 3). It appears that the use of pragmatic flexibility types is higher in mothers with HEB in comparison of that with mothers of LEB.

Despite significant differences, both HEB and LEB mothers have a tendency to use certain types of pragmatic flexibility with children aged 3 to 6. They tend to use more frequently the four types of Negotiating the immediate activity with Request and proposal (NIA: RP); Discussing a joint focus of attention with stating a declarative statement (DJF: ST), or with asking a wh-question (DJF: QN), or with asking a yes/no question (DJF: YQ) in their interaction with children. This implies a certain manner in which the mothers lead the interaction with children in a Chinese cultural context. Both HEB and LEB mothers tend to use a request or a proposal to negotiate their next activity, and to use a declarative statement, or wh and y/n questions to focus children's attention. It seems that their educational backgrounds did not influence this leading behaviour of mothers in interaction with their children.

Table 3. Frequency of pragmatic flexibility types used by mothers with different educational backgrounds (%)

Pragmatic flexibility types	Age range													
	36M		42M		48M		54M		60M		66M		72M	
	H	L	H	L	H	L	H	L	H	L	H	L	H	L
NIA:RP	21.2	18.8	21.1	19.8	20.3	16.4	19.1	23.5	17.3	16.4	14.2	11.6	13.9	19.8
DJF:ST	8.0	10.9	7.8	7.6	10.8	9.6	11.5	13.5	9.6	10.6	11.2	10.6	8.4	14.8
DJF:QN	11.1	7.5	9.8	7.9	8.1	10.1	6.7	7.7	8.9	5.9	9.0	12.2	8.4	8.5
DJF:YQ	6.6	7.0	6.2	6.5	4.8	7.4	7.4	7.6	6.5	5.8	7.0	7.3	7.0	6.5
TXT:TX	.51	1.9	5.0	3.0	2.9	5.6	7.0	5.2	8.4	5.8	10.1	7.6	7.6	4.0
DCA:AB	.13	1.0	2.0	.83	3.0	.28	2.4	2.7	.40	.12	1.1	2.3	.83	1.4
DCC:RT	2.0	2.8	2.7	1.7	1.8	3.1	2.0	1.4	1.9	1.4	2.4	4.6	2.9	2.9
DCC:YQ	2.2	2.8	1.4	1.8	1.2	2.0	.87	.94	.99	2.2	.86	1.7	1.7	.78
DHA:QN	2.3	2.6	2.3	2.4	.86	1.5	.51	1.0	1.5	2.9	.27	.92	.37	.66
DHA:RP	2.0	1.8	1.1	2.8	1.7	1.8	1.7	1.8	2.8	3.0	1.1	1.0	.95	.96
DHA:ST	.93	1.3	.66	1.9	1.1	.88	.71	2.1	1.8	1.8	.93	1.2	1.0	1.2
DJF:AB	1.6	.46	.46	.25	.68	.14	.55	0	1.2	2.4	.13	.18	.17	.12
DJF:AC	.51	.50	.14	1.2	.83	2.7	1.5	1.2	0	.55	.33	.61	1.9	5.1
DJF:EQ	1.7	.46	1.4	.92	1.8	2.0	1.1	1.5	1.7	1.8	1.8	1.3	1.3	1.5
DJF:MK	.51	.31	.56	.46	1.2	.78	1.0	.86	1.1	2.0	1.4	1.5	1.2	.66
DJF:RP	1.1	2.1	2.5	2.4	2.0	1.6	1.3	3.1	2.2	2.7	5.2	1.3	2.4	1.9
DJF:SA	2.5	1.5	1.7	2.2	1.4	1.8	1.9	2.7	1.8	1.8	2.3	3.0	1.7	3.0
MRK:MK	1.5	.38	.56	1.2	.43	.57	.24	.10	1.5	1.8	.66	1.1	.37	.12
NIA:QN	3.2	2.4	2.2	2.8	3.8	1.7	2.8	3.0	2.0	1.5	1.9	1.3	1.7	3.3
NIA:RQ	3.6	3.5	2.7	2.4	2.5	3.2	2.3	1.0	1.5	1.3	.80	1.4	.79	.42

3.3 Comparison of language quality in interaction by HEB and LEB mothers

3.3.1 *Analysis of language input in interaction with children by HEB and LEB mothers*

In examining the language quality of HEB and LEB mothers' input, the analysis has used Mean Length Utterance (MLU), the MLU of the 5 longest utterances (MLU5), tokens and types of vocabulary and the size of the vocabulary in interaction to measure their linguistic productivity and language use. In all these four aspects, HEB mothers appear to have a statistically higher input with their children than LEB mothers, according to a One-Way Analysis of Covariance (ANCOVA) (see Table 4), i.e. HEB mothers employed a longer MLU, longer MLU5 and used a greater variety and size of vocabulary in their conversations with their children.

Table 4. Descriptive Statistics of language input by HEB and LEB mothers

Items	HEB (N=70)		LEB (N=70)		ANCOVA[a]		
	M	*SD*	*M*	*SD*	*df*	*F*	*P*
MLU	3.68	.44	3.43	.45	1	11.918	.001**
MLU5 (MLU of the 5 longest utterances)	10.74	1.62	10.03	1.82	1	5.744	.018*
Vocabulary types	282.0	75.75	237.6	74.35	1	12.353	.001**
Vocabulary tokens	1088.4	468.8	919.2	479.7	1	4.981	.027*

3.3.2 *Analysis of language types used in speech acts by HEB and LEB mothers*

Looking further at the data (Table 5), differences are found in the language ability used in speech act types in mother–child interactions by HEB and LEB mothers. In the four most frequently used syntactic structure types: statement, request/proposal, wh-question and yes/no question utterances, HEB and LEB mothers showed significant differences in MLU, MLU5, variety of vocabulary and total vocabulary (see *p* values for ANCOVA in right hand column). HEB mothers have shown a higher use and wider range than LEB mothers in most of these four types. This implies that there are qualitative differences between the two groups of mothers in their language input to their children.

3.3.3 *Analysis of mean length of turns within a topic in mother–child interactions*

The mean length of turns refers here to the average number of a cluster of utterances in several turns spoken between a child and a parent on the same topic in their interactions. The number of utterances used was calculated to find out the average number of these utterances in the mean length of turns and the vocabulary

Table 5. Comparison of key speech act types in utterance length and vocabulary size by HEB and LEB mothers

Items		HEB (N = 70)		LEB (N = 70)		ANCOVA[a]		
		M	*SD*	*M*	*SD*	*df*	*F*	*P*
MLU	Statement	4.372	.75	4.000	.76	1	8.736	.004**
	Request/prop.	3.869	.57	3.545	.56	1	11.589	.001**
	Wh-question	4.652	.61	4.249	.51	1	17.712	.000**
	Y/N question	5.101	.78	4.521	.84	1	18.315	.000**
MLU5	Statement	8.463	2.16	7.84	2.09	1	3.017	.085
	Request/prop.	7.939	1.61	7.21	1.59	1	7.337	.008**
	Wh-question	7.849	1.70	6.757	1.54	1	15.649	.000**
	Y/N question	9.095	1.84	7.861	2.36	1	12.096	.001**
Vocabulary tokens	Statement	96.83	46.76	84.11	44.94	1	2.623	.108
	Request/prop.	92.43	33.08	75.89	31.51	1	9.807	.002**
	Wh-question	67.52	27.01	52.01	25.83	1	12.109	.001**
	Y/N question	69.39	26.43	59.50	32.66	1	3.941	.049*
Vocabulary types	Statement	189.52	126.16	163.83	115.89	1	1.557	.214
	Request/prop.	226.48	118.14	183.30	119.55	1	4.994	.027*
	Wh-question	185.18	109.30	149.60	104.25	1	4.007	.047*
	Y/N question	166.22	84.94	142.84	109.92	1	1.554	.160

size was calculated. Figure 4 shows that there is no statistical significance for the utterance numbers in the mean length of turns produced by HEB and LEB mothers in their interaction with children.

However, the number of vocabulary items used in the mean length of turns shows a significant statistical difference (see Figure 5). This suggests that there are more words used in the mean length of turns by HEB mothers than by LEB mothers, especially with the group of children aged 4. For children aged 6 and 7, it seems that HEB and LEB mothers used a similar number of words in interaction with their children.

The data in Figures 4, 5 and Table 6 show that there are differences in the language provided to children by HEB and LEB mothers in their interactions and the HEB mothers appear to show a higher ability in providing syntactic and semantic input to their children. Thus, even though it is considered that the speech acts provided to children appear to be similar between HEB and LEB mothers, the quality of the language input is different between them. These differences may have an impact on the language development of children.

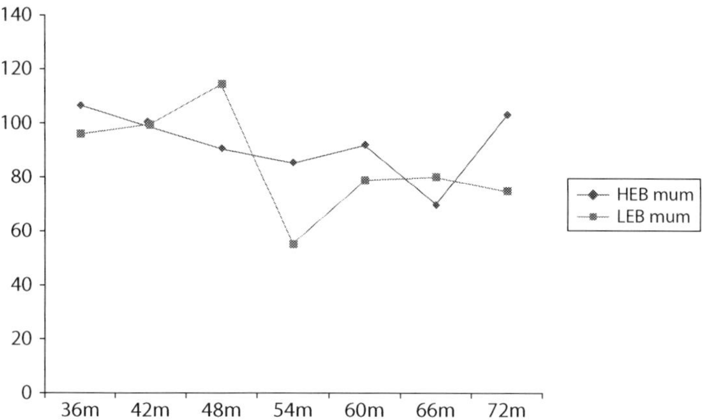

Figure 4. comparison of the number of utterances in the mean length of turns by HEB and LEB mothers

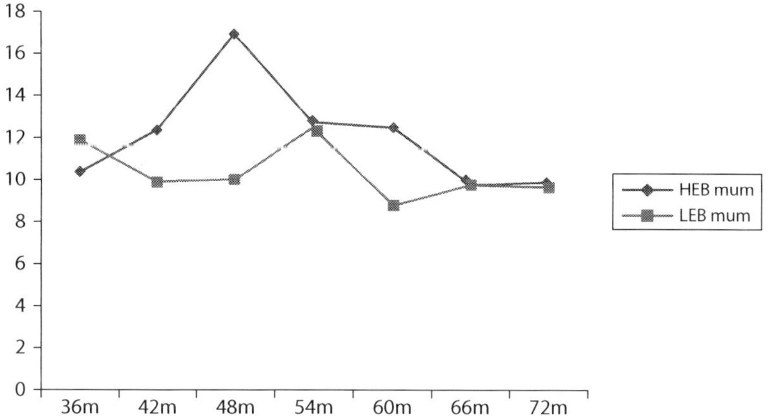

Figure 5. comparison of size of vocabulary in the mean length of turns used by HEB and LEB mothers

Table 6. Data analysis of the average number of utterances and vocabulary size in an exchange of turns by HEB and LEB mothers

Item in an exchange of turns	HEB (N = 70)		LEB (N = 70)		ANCOVA[a]		
	M	SD	M	SD	df	F	P
Averaged number of utterances	92.24	30.43	91.08	36.15	1	.044	.834
Averaged number of vocabulary items	12.08	4.13	10.34	4.04	1	6.403	.013*

4. Discussion and conclusion

This chapter focused on the interaction between mothers and children in the Chinese context and analysed the similarity and differences between HEB and LEB mothers in their interactions with children. It has examined and compared the quantity and quality of social interchange, speech act and pragmatic flexibility by HEB and LEB mothers with their children. The main findings are summarised and discussed below.

Firstly, mothers, despite their diverse educational backgrounds, show more similarities than differences in the way they interact with their children. There is no statistical difference in language use in general between HEB and LEB mothers. There are similar language use patterns in both groups with the most frequently used types of social interchanges and speech acts.

This suggests that there is a good level of cultural consistency between HEB and LEB mothers in their way of using language in mother–child interaction. They appear to use similar social interchange patterns, speech act types and the most frequently used pragmatic flexibility items. For social interchanges, both groups have used certain communicative acts more frequently, e.g. both mother and child discussed activities with a joint focus of attention (DJF); they negotiated their immediate activities (NIA) and directed hearer's attention (DHA). These results may imply that both groups of mothers expect children to carry out activities in a sustained way with a relatively long time of focused attention. Similarly, certain speech act types have been used with a high frequency by both groups of mothers in their interactional activities with children, e.g. giving suggestions to the child regarding what to do or not to do (RP), using wh-questions (QN) or using yes or no questions (YQ) to find out the child's understanding or request. This way of using these speech acts may indicate a strong directive function of language use. These Chinese children seem to be in a responsive mode to answer questions put to them or to react to their mother's suggestions, requests or directives. This behaviour could indicate a special Chinese approach to mother–child interaction patterns and functions in a Chinese cultural context in which a child is expected to be led and directed by a parent and a young person should listen to an older one. This special feature may also imply that the interactive process seems to be controlled by the mother, even though the child is the focus of the attention, as pointed out by previous studies in China (Yue et al. 1997; Zhou 2002).

Nevertheless, some differences do exist in quality and quantity of language input by HEB and LEB mothers in their interaction with children. These differences can be found in the frequency of speech acts: more were used by HEB mothers. This suggests HEB mothers may participate more in interactive activities, which might well provide more cognitive stimulus to their children. At the same time, other differences can be identified in utterance length and vocabulary size in inter-active speech acts. Again, HEB mothers appear to offer more variety of vocabulary, longer utterances with more words, and a longer discussion within an exchange of turns on the same topic. This facilitates the realization of pragmatic flexibility in their interaction with children, probably because the HEB mothers may have richer knowledge and a better awareness of the educational purpose of interactions due to their own previous higher educational experience. This difference in qualitative and quantitative language input between HEB and LEB mothers may lead to differences in child language development in the long run, even though there are similar speech act patterns offered by both groups of mothers to their children. Understanding the relationship between mothers' input and language development is the first step towards understanding of mothers' role in children's educational attainment.

In conclusion, this chapter investigated features of language use among Mandarin-speaking mothers and children. While there are differences between mothers of different social and educational backgrounds regarding utterance length and vocabulary size, the data show more similarities than differences among Mandarin-speaking mothers, suggesting a good level of cultural consistency among Chinese mothers under study. Further studies are needed to see how Chinese cultures of learning (Cortazzi & Jin 2002, Jin & Cortazzi 2011) can facilitate mother–child interaction and enhance child language development and what can be learned from other cultures to help Chinese parents to enrich Chinese patterns of interaction and learning.

References

Anderson, Elaine. S. 1990. *Speaking with Style, the sociolinguistic skills of children*. London: Routledge.

Atkinson, Paul. 1985. *Language, Structure and Reproduction, an introduction to the sociology of Basil Bernstein*. London: Methuen.

Bernstein, Basil. 1971; 1973. *Class, Codes and Control*. Vol.1; Vol.2. London: Routledge,

Bernstein, Basil. 1994. "Edwards and his Language Codes: Response to A.D. Edwards, Language Codes and Classroom Practice". *Oxford Review of Education* 20:2. 173–182.

Cortazzi, Martin & Jin, Lixian 2002. "Cultures of Learning, the social construction of educational identities". *Discourses in Search of Members*, ed. by David. C. S. Li. 49–78. New York: University Press of America.

De Villiers, Jill G. & Peter A. De Villiers. 1978. *Language Acquisition*. Cambridge, MA: Harvard University Press.

Desforges, Charles. 2003. *The Impact of Parental Involvement, Parental Support and Family Education on Pupil Achievements and Adjustment: A Literature Review*. London: DfES Publications

Dittmar, Norbert. 1976. *Sociolinguistics, a critical survey of theory and application*. London: Edward Arnold.

Edwards, Anthony Davies. 1976. *Language in Culture and Class*. London: Heinemann.

Edwards, John R. 1979. *Language and Disadvantage*. London: Edward Arnold.

Fasold, Ralph. 1990. *The Sociolinguistics of Language*. Oxford: Basil Blackwell.

Gordon, John C. B. 1981. *Verbal Deficit, a critique*. London: Croom Helm.

Giles, Howard. & Peter F. Powesland. 1975. *Speech Style and Social Evaluation*. London: Academic Press.

Halliday, Michael A. K. 1978. *Language as Social Semiotic*, London: Edward Arnold.

Hammer, Scheffner Carol & Weiss, Amy. 1999. "Guiding language development: How African American mothers and their infants structure play interactions". *Journal of Speech, Language and Hearing Research* 42.1219–1233

Hart, Betty & Todd R. Risley. 1995. *Meaningful differences in everyday experience of young American children*. Baltimore: Paul Brookes Publishing Co.

Hiromi, Tsjui. 2002. "Young Children Expressing their Communicative Intents: A preliminary study of the interactions between Japanese children and their caregivers". *The journal of Doctoral Research in Education* 2.72–84.

Hoff, Erika, Laursen, Brett & Twila, Tardiff. 2002. "Socioeconomic status and parenting". *Handbook of parenting, Volume II: Ecology & biology of parenting* ed. by Marc H. Bornstein. 161–188. Mahwah, NJ: Lawrence Erlbaum Associates.

Hoff, Erika & Letitia, Naigles. 2002. "How children use input to acquire a lexicon". *Child Development*. 73.418–433.

Hoff, Erika & Chunyan, Tian. 2005. "Socioeconomic status and cultural influences on language". *Journal of Communication Disorders* 38. 271–278.

Huang, Chiung-chih. 2011. Referential choice and informativeness in mother–child conversation: A focus on the mother. *Language Sciences*. doi:https://sslvpn.nccu.edu.tw/10.1016/,DanaInfo=dx.doi.org+j.langsci.2011.10.003

Jin, Lixian & Martin, Cortazzi. eds. 2011. *Researching Chinese Learners: skills, perceptions, intercultural adaptations*. Houndmills: Palgrave, Macmillan.

Jing-Schmidt, Zhuo. 2012 "Maternal affective speech in mother–child interaction: A cross-cultural perspective". *Chinese Language and Discourse* 3:1. 57–89.

Keşli, Yeşim. 2006. *The Impact of Birth Order and Gender On Pragmatic Development Of Turkish Children In L1 Acquisition*. Unpublished PhD Dissertation. Adana: Çukurova University.

MacWhinney, Brian. 1991. *The CHILDES project: Computational tools for analyzing talk*. Hillsdale, NJ: Erlbaum.

MacWhinney, Brian & Harry, Osser. 1977. "Verbal planning function in children's speech". *Child Development* 48.978–985.

MacWhinney, Brian & Catherine, Snow. 1985. "The child language data exchange system". *Journal of Child Language* 12.271–295.

MacWhinney, Brian & Catherine, Snow. 1990. "The child language date exchange system: An update". *Journal of Child Language*. 17.457–472.

Mahoney, Gerald, Boyce, Glenn, Fewell, Rebecca, Spiker, Donna & C. Abigail, Wheeden. 1998. "The Relationship of Parent–Child Interaction to the Effectiveness of Early Intervention Services for at-Risk Children and Children with Disabilities". *Topics in Early Childhood Special Education* 18. 15–17.

Ninio, Anat, Wheeler, Polly, Snow, Catherine, Pan, Barbara, A. & Pamela R, Rollins. 1990. *Inventory of Communicative Acts- Abridged (INCA-A): A coding manual.* Unpublished Manuscript, Harvard Graduate School of Education.

Ninio, Anat & Catherine, Snow. 1996. *Pragmatic Development.* Colorado: Westview Press, Inc.

Robinson, Peter. 1978. *Language Management in Education, the Australian context.* Sydney: George Allen & Unwin.

Romaine, Jennifer. 1984. *The Language of Children and Adolescents, the acquisition of communicative competence.* Oxford: Basil Blackwell.

Stubbs, Michael. 1986. *Educational Linguistics.* Oxford: Basil Blackwell.

Trudgill, Peter. 1974. *Sociolinguistics, an introduction to language and society.* Harmondsworth: Penguin Books.

Trudgill, Peter. 1975. *Accent, Dialect and the School.* London: Edward Arnold.

Wardhaugh, Ronald. 1992. *An Introduction to Sociolinguistics.* Oxford: Blackwell.

Zhou, Jing. 2002. *Pragmatic Development of Mandarin-speaking Children.* Nanjing: Nanjing Normal University Press.

乐国安, D.G. 弗里德曼, C. 帕克: 中国的母子关系模式及文化传递, 《天津师范大学学报》(社会科学版), 1997年第3期。 [Yue, Guoan, Freidman, D.G., Park, C. 1997. "Chinese mother and child relationship patterns and cultural transfer". *Tianjin Normal University Journal (Social Science Volume).* Vol. 3.]

Chinese preschool children's comprehension of a picture storybook*

Linhui Li, Jing Zhou, Baogen Liu and Xiaomei Gao
Shanghai Normal University / East China Normal University / Hangzhou
Kindergarten Teacher College, Zhejiang Normal University / Zizhu
Kindergarten attached to East China Normal University

This chapter explores 3 to 6 year old Chinese children's comprehension of a
picture storybook *The Very Hungry Caterpillar*. The results show: (1) Chinese
children's understanding of images, actions and characters' states improves
with age; (2) Children develop their understanding of images first, followed by
actions and then characters' states; (3) It is easier for children to understand images prominent in pictures than those not prominent in pictures or containing
culture-specific information with which children are not familiar, actions represented directly through the relationship of different images than those actions
which require making a connection with preceding and following pictures, and
characters' states represented by visible information such as size and colour than
those less visible or age-appropriate.

1.   Introduction and background

Multiliteracy entails understanding and creation of meaning through composition of different semiotic symbols such as language, visual images, audio signals,
gestures, spaces and so on (Cope & Kalantzis, 2000; 2009). Among these different
components, children's visual literacy, i.e. the ability to understand and communicate meaning represented by pictures, has drawn more and more attention in

* This chapter is one of the outcomes of "From Image to Print: Research on the Process of
Acquisition of Chinese Characters by Chinese children", a Program funded by the Key Human
and Social Science Research bases of Ministry of Education, China (07JJDXLX264). The first
author would like to acknowledge the sponsorship by "Doctoral Student's Academic Visiting
Abroad Foundation" of East China Normal University and Centre for Intercultural Research in
Communication and Learning of De Montfort University, UK. Permission for reproduction of
images from *The Very Hungary Caterpillar* is given by the publisher.

the field in recent years (Edwards & Willis, 2000; Williams, 2007; Cooper, 2008; Woolley, 2010). However, many studies available to date either focus only on children's perception of a single visual component such as shape, line and colour, or the way that pictures or illustrations motivate children to read and help them to understand the meaning of text (Nicholas, 2007). Issues such as children's comprehension of narrative meaning through pictures and children's meaning making through the interaction of pictures and text when they read a storybook are largely ignored due to a number of challenges. First, pictures and words interact in different ways (Nikolajeva, 2006). So far, five types of interaction between pictures and words have been identified. They are symmetry, enhancement, complementarity, counterpoint and contradiction (Nikolajeva & Scott, 2000). Secondly, reading comprehension is a very complicated process (Kintsch & Rawson, 2005; Kang, 2007) and it is even more difficult to assess reading comprehension of preschool children who cannot read or write words (Bourg, et al., 1997).

In this chapter, we first discuss the importance of pictures in children's comprehension of a storybook. We then look into 'story grammar' and 'grammar of visual design' and how these two concepts help us understand the process of comprehension of a picture storybook. In the data section, we report the results of a study on preschool children's comprehension of Eric Carle's well-known picture storybook *The Very Hungry Caterpillar* (2008) through three analytical measures. Finally we discuss the general features of children's comprehension of a storybook.

1.1   Eye tracking evidence for the role of pictures in children's reading comprehension

In recent years, the invention of eye tracking machines has made it feasible to record children's visual fixations, i.e. eye movements, at regular intervals when reading a picture storybook. Through eye movement studies, it is found that children pay more attention to pictures than to print and that pictures and illustrations serve as the main visual information resources for young children in their comprehension of narrative meaning when reading together with adults or reading alone. Justice and Lankford (2002) and Justice et al. (2005) used two picture books in their experiment, one with prominent print and the other without. The result showed that children aged from 52 to 68 months barely examined print. When they read the book with prominent print, they only spent 5.6% of the total amount of time on print. This result is consistent with the findings of the studies reported by Evans and Saint-Aubin (2005). In their studies, two groups of children (five children aged 48–61 months and 10 children aged 52–60 months) were asked to read five books which differed in the proportion of print against illustration. The result showed that children spent little time on print regardless of the nature of text and illustration, and even when they were given additional time, children's attention was still fixed on pictures. This seems to be the case with older children too. Roy-Charland, Saint-Aubin and Evans (2007) observed eye movements of 30 children from kindergarten to Grade 4 and found children who could read still spent nearly half of the time on illustrations.

Research also shows an age effect in the amount of time children spend on print vs. pictures. While children spend time mainly on pictures during reading, they look at print for a longer time as age increases. Gao (2009) measured eye movements of 162 Chinese children aged from 3 to 6 years when they read the picture storybook *The Very Hungry Caterpillar* alone. The percentages of time children spent on print at age 3, 4, 5 and 6 were 1.08%, 3.11%, 9.2% and 18.48% respectively. Gao suggested that children might follow a sequence of developmental stages in picture storybook reading. They might construct meaning by reading pictures only at a younger age, then by reading pictures and text separately as they grow older, and then finally by reading pictures and text interactively.

1.2 The role of two 'grammars' in children's comprehension of a picture storybook

A limited number of studies attempted to understand young children's reading comprehension of a storybook through the concept of "story grammar", which was proposed initially by Rumelhart (1975, 1977), and further developed by Mandler and Johnson (1977), Thorndyke (1977), Glenn (1978), and Stein and Glenn (1979) (for a review, see Lu & Peng, 1990; Cortazzi, 2002). A typical story grammar consists of six main narrative elements: setting, characters, goal/initiating event, problem/episodes, solution, and resolution/ending (Mandler and Johnson's model, 1977). Story grammar proves to be a useful analytical tool in understanding children's reading comprehension. For example, Paris and Paris (2003) developed a "narrative comprehension task" to examine pictorial comprehension of children from kindergarten to Grade 2 in their longitudinal research. In their study, story grammar was used to analyse stories retold by children after reading a storybook without print. They found that kindergarten children aged 5 to 6 could only tell about two components of the story grammar. The components they found easier to tell are setting and initiating event. The percentages of children who could tell the other four components were very low. Lin (1999) also used story retelling as one of the tasks to investigate the story comprehension of 60 Taiwan children aged 5 to 6 years. She argued that for different storybooks children may tell different story grammar components. Wagner et al. (1999) compared story comprehension of SLI (specific language impairment) children aged 5 with that of typically developing children aged 4 to 5;8 years in Sweden. Using Stein and Glenn's story grammar model, which includes seven items, i.e., setting, initiating event, response state, response plan, attempt, consequence and resolution / reaction, they analysed the children's retold stories and found that SLI children could tell significantly fewer components than normally developing children. They concluded that SLI children have difficulty in understanding the story through pictures in addition to their language impairment.

While story grammar has proved useful in understanding how children comprehend narrative stories in general, 'grammar of visual design' provides "a useful framework for thinking about the different kinds of meanings that images contribute to stories" (Unsworth & Wheeler, 2002:68). The concept of 'grammar of visual design' was proposed by Kress and Van Leeuwen (1996) in their book *Reading Images: The Grammar of Visual Design*. Kress and Van Leeuwen argued that "visual structures realize meaning as linguistics structures do, and thereby point to different interpretations of experience and different forms of social interaction" (p. 2). Following the tradition of systemic functional linguistics, they suggested that three different kinds of meaning should always be made simultaneously (Kress & Van Leeuwen, 1996; Jewitt & Oyama, 2001; Unsworth & Wheeler, 2002). These are:

– Representational meaning, which is "first of all conveyed by the (abstract or concrete) 'participants' (people, places or things) depicted" (Jewitt & Oyama, 2001, p. 141). Visual participants relate to each other in two patterns: concept pattern and narrative pattern. In the former, participants are defined or classified as being or meaning something, belonging to a certain category, or having certain characteristics or components. In the latter, participants connect in terms of "doings" and "happenings", and thus represent the actions, events or processes of change.
– Interactive meaning, which is constructed between viewers and the world represented in a picture, an interface through which readers construct what is represented. Factors such as distance, contact and point of view influence the construction of interactive meanings.
– Compositional meanings, which are conveyed by layout of an image indicating information value or relative emphasis among the components of the image. Factors such as location, size and border of participants influence the way attention is given to various aspects of the image.

Most of spatial "syntax" is usually described in formalist and aesthetic terms such as lines, colours, shapes, etc., and analysts do not look at how these contribute to representational meaning (Schwarcz, 1982; Nodelman, 1988; Doonan, 1993; Stewig, 1995; Jewitt & Oyama, 2001). In contrast, 'grammar of visual design' incorporates image into the process of meaning making (Jewitt & Oyama, 2001).

According to 'grammar of visual design', participants are basic units for meaningful representation of images and it is through the relationship between participants that we understand what is done or what is happening. In the next section, we will look at a way to integrate 'grammar of visual design' and 'story grammar' in order to understand children's comprehension of picture storybook reading.

1.3   A framework for estimating children's comprehension of picture storybook reading

Although 'grammar of visual design' and 'story grammar' were developed for different purposes, they essentially look at the same things from different angles. For example, setting and character in story grammar are equivalent to participants such as places, things, people or animals in grammar of visual design; goal/initiating event, problem/episodes, solution, and resolution/ending in story grammar are represented by relationships between participants in grammar of visual design; how characters feel in story grammar is in fact 'interactive meaning' in grammar of visual design, through which readers' points of view and experience interact with the meaning represented through pictures. To integrate these two analytical tools, we propose the following three analytical measures to investigate children's comprehension of picture storybooks (Figure 1).

– Image of participant: To investigate whether children can recognize characters and things which represent the objects, place or time in a storybook.
– Action event: To investigate whether children can understand what is happening in a storybook by reasoning about the relationship between participants.
– State of character: To investigate whether children can make interactive and compositional meaning from pictures in order to know what a character looks like or how a character feels.

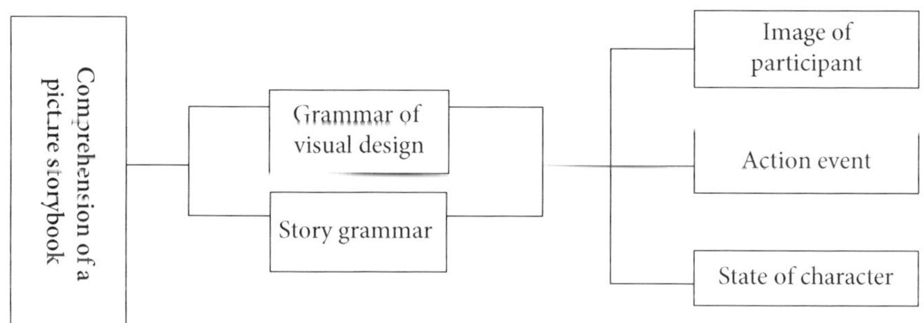

Figure 1.   A framework for investigating children's comprehension of picture storybook reading

2. Method

2.1 Research participants

120 typically developing children from five kindergartens in Shanghai, China took part initially in the study between September and December 2008. The children were randomly selected and permission was sought from their parents or guardians. Their ages ranged from 3 to 6 years. There were equal numbers of children in each age group (n = 30), and equal numbers of boys (n = 60) and girls (n = 60). Two children aged 3, one child aged 4 and one child aged 5 could not retell the story and were therefore excluded from the data analysis. The final number of participants was 116 children.

2.2 Materials

The book used in this study was the Chinese version of *The Very Hungry Caterpillar* (Carle 2008). This well-known storybook, originally published in English and

Table 1. Words about image of participant (IOP), action event (AE) and state of character (SOC) in the storybook

Page	IOP	AE	SOC
P5	egg, moon, leaf	lay on	little
P6	caterpillar, sun	came out of	tiny and very hungry
P7	caterpillar, apple, sun	look for, ate	hungry
P8	caterpillar, pear	ate	hungry
P9	caterpillar, plum	ate	hungry
P10	caterpillar, strawberry	ate	hungry
P11	caterpillar, orange	ate	hungry
P12	caterpillar, chocolate cake, ice-cream, pickle, cheese, salami, lollipop, cherry pie, sausage, cupcake, watermelon	ate	stomachache
P13	caterpillar, leaf	ate	feel better
P14	caterpillar, cocoon	built, surround, stay inside, nibble, push way out	big and fat
P15	butterfly	become[a]	beautiful
Scores	32	16	11

[a] The word "was" in the original English version was translated into "变成", meaning 'become' in the Chinese version.

then translated into 47 languages, is popular among children. In addition, in the storybook, "pictures and words are telling the same story" (Gao, 2009: 38), which makes it easy for children who can not read words to construct story meaning from the pictures. All the words in the text of storybook are classified into image of participant (IOP), action event (AE) and state of character (SOC), as shown in the table below (Table 1).

2.3 Procedure

Before the story retelling task started, a researcher engaged each child in playing with a doll for a few minutes to warm up. Then the researcher gave the instruction "Qiaohu /Dora (both are the names of popular cartoon characters in China) would like you to tell him/her a story. Would you please read this book first and then tell him/her?" After the child read the book, the researcher asked the child to retell the story with the book in front of him/her. During the retelling, the researcher prompted the child to continue the story with questions such as "then what happened?", but did not mention or answer the child's questions about the content of the story.

2.4 Data analysis

The utterances by the children and the researcher in the story retelling task were transcribed into CHAT files following the format defined for the Child Language Data Exchange System (CHILDES) (MacWhinney 1991). Children's statements about IOP, AE and SOC were first sorted in the CLAN (Child Language Analysis) program, and then a score of 1, 0.5 or 0 was given depending on how accurately they understood image of participant, action event and state of character according to the words in Table 1. For example, if a child said "a tiny caterpillar came" about page 6, he/she would get 1 for "caterpillar", 0.5 for "tiny" and 0.5 for "came" compared with the original words "caterpillar", "came out of" and "tiny and hungry". Since the child did not mention the "sun", he / she would get a score of 0 for this word.

As seen in Table 1, the possible total scores of IOP, AE and SOC are different. Both the total scores and percentage score were calculated and analyzed in SPSS16.0. For example, the total score of IOP for a child is the sum of all scores a child got for words of IOP; the percentage score for a child is the total score of IOP divided by the full mark 32. The percentage scores for IOP, AE and SOC were then compared.

3. Results

3.1 Overview of children's comprehension

As shown in Table 2, the means of scores and percentage score of children's comprehension of IOP, AE, and SOC increase with age. One-way ANOVA analysis found a significant age effect on comprehension of IOP, AE and SOC (df = 3, F = 301.312, p = .00; df = 3, F = 266.740, p = .00; df = 3, F = 68.794, P = .00) Post Hoc analysis shows that differences in IOP and AE are highly significant between age groups of 3, 4, 5 and 6 years (p = .00); the difference in children's comprehension of SOC is highly significant between age groups of 3, 4 and 5 years (p = .00), but is not significant between age groups of 5 and 6 years.

Table 2. Comprehension of the Story by Different Age Groups

Age group	IOP		AE		SOC	
	Mean of score	Mean of Percentage score	Mean of score	Mean of Percentage score	Mean of score	Mean of Percentage score
3	4.236	0.132	0.587	0.037	0.039	0.004
4	10.282	0.321	3.475	0.217	1.393	0.127
5	13.402	0.419	6.143	0.384	2.747	0.250
6	16.861	0.527	7.674	0.480	2.995	0.272
Mean	11.312	0.354	4.531	0.283	1.820	0.165
F test	301.312***		266.740***		68.794***	

* < .05; ** < .01; *** < .001

3.2 Comparison between IOP, AE and SOC

A Pair-wise T test was used to analyze the difference between percentage scores of IOP, AE and SOC among all age groups (Table 3, Figure 1).

The results show that children's percentage scores of SOC are significantly lower than that of AE, which is in turn significantly lower than that of IOP. Children of 3 years old get very low percentage scores of AE and SOC, as low as zero in the case of SOC. From 4 years old, children's percentage scores of AE and SOC start to increase. With age, the difference between children's percentage scores of IOP and AE is smaller. However, the difference between children's percentage scores of SOC and that of IOP and AE increases with age.

Table 3. Comparison of percentage score by different measures

		IOP	AE	SOC
	3	t = 16.111 ***		
AE	4	t = 9.044 ***		
	5	t = 3.589 ***		
	6	t = 6.126 ***		
SOC	3		t = 4.604 ***	
	4		t = 9.989 ***	
	5		t = 10.478 ***	
	6		t = 17.679 ***	
IOP	3			t = 19.030 ***
	4			t = 13.910 ***
	5			t = 13.653 ***
	6			t = 23.221 ***

* < .05; ** < .01; *** < .001

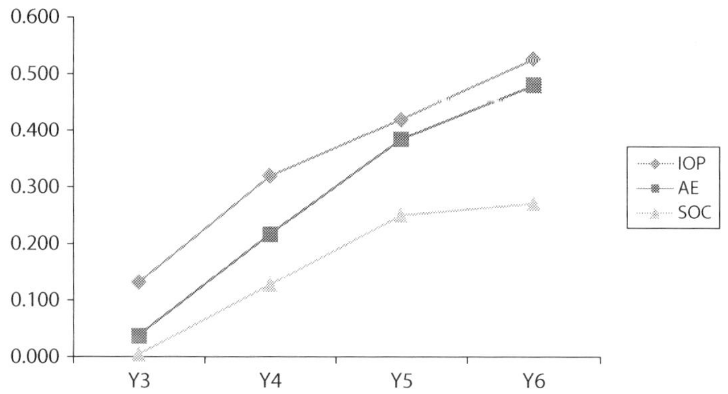

Figure 1. Comparison of percentage score by different items

3.3 Children's comprehension in each analytical measure

3.3.1 *Image of participant (IOP)*

All participants in the story book *The Very Hungry Caterpillar* can be divided into two types, a protagonist and an object. There are three different images of protagonist. egg, caterpillar and butterfly. Figure 2 provides an overview of children's scores of accuracy in their retelling. Older children get higher scores than younger children for all three images. Children in different age groups understand the three images in a similar way: egg is least understood, caterpillar more so, and butterfly most accurately understood. The means of scores through all age groups are 0.215, 0.386 and 0.806 respectively for egg, caterpillar and butterfly.

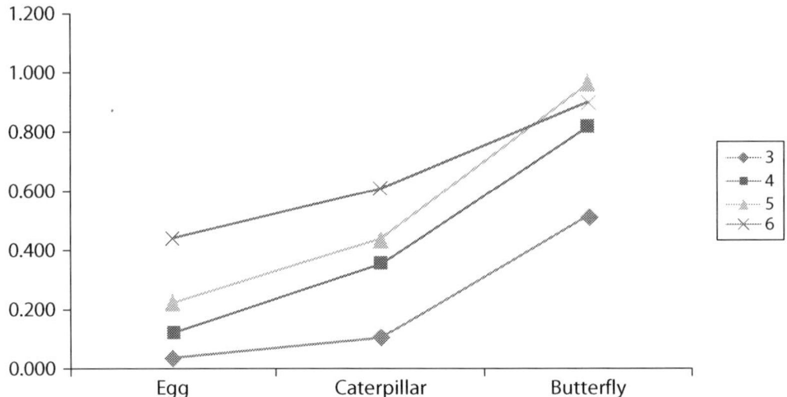

Figure 2. Comparison of score by different IOP- A

There are 21 object participants in the book (Figures 3 and 4). Similarities are observed among children of four age groups in their scores of accuracy. For example, all age groups get higher average scores for images of *strawberry, leaf 2, pear, apple, sun, moon, lollipop* and *watermelon*, which are 0.787, 0.696, 0.681, 0.677, 0.427, 0.400, 0.379, 0.338 and 0.315 respectively. In contrast, they get lower average scores for images of *chocolate cake, leaf, salami, cheese, cocoon, ice-cream, cupcake, plum, pickle, sausage* and *cherry pie*, which are 0.209, 0.200, 0.196, 0.192, 0.172, 0.169, 0.161, 0.133, 0.116, 0.104 and 0.049 respectively. In contrast, this pattern suggests a high degree of consistency in children's comprehension of storybooks and shows that there are some images that children can understand more easily than others.

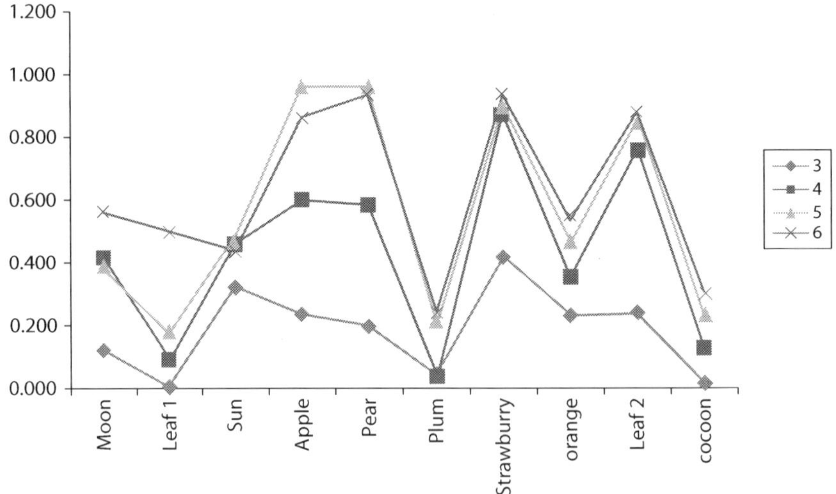

Figure 3. Comparison of score by different IOP- B

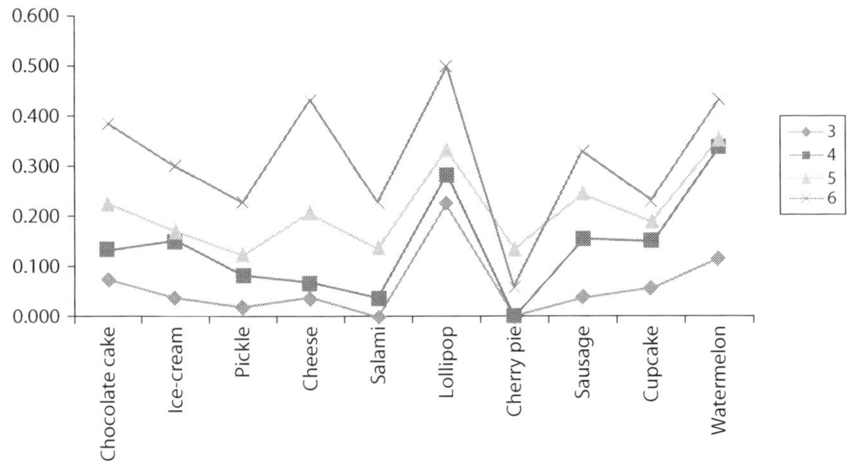

Figure 4. Comparison of score by different IOP-C

3.3.2   *Action event (AE)*

There are 16 action events in the book *The Very Hungry Caterpillar* (the verb 'ate' was repeated seven times and therefore its score of accuracy is the average of scores over seven times). Figure 5 shows the average scores of different AE by each age group. As children get older, they get higher scores for AEs. Similar to IOP, children in different age groups also show a good level of consistency. They achieve the highest scores for *'ate'* and *'become'*, 0.488 and 0.422 respectively; lower scores of less than 0.200 for *'came out of'*, *'look for'*, *'built'*; and the lowest scores of less than 0.100 for *'lay on'*, *'surround'*, *'stay inside'*, *'nibble'*, and *'push way out'*.

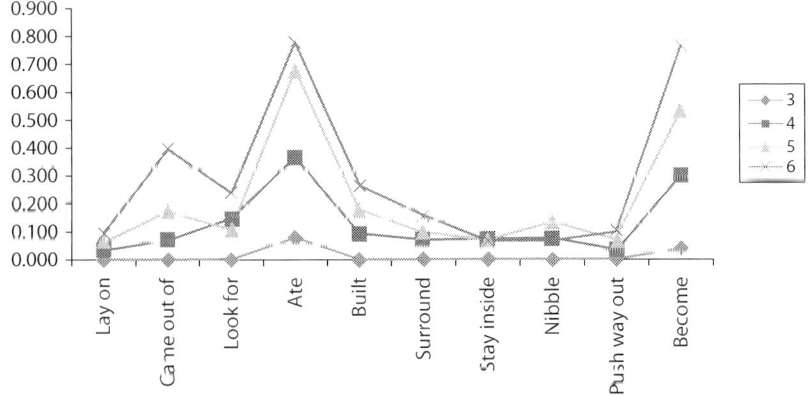

Figure 5. Comparison of score by different AEs

3.3.3 *State of Character (SOC)*

There are 11 states of character in the story book ('*hungry*' is repeated over five times and its score of accuracy is the average of scores over five times). Figure 6 shows the average scores of different SOCs by each age group. There is a clear age effect in that three year old children know very little about states of character. As children get older they get higher scores for these SOC. Children from different age groups, with the exception of the age group of three, seem to develop understanding of SOC in a similar way: higher scores for '*beautiful*', '*big and fat*', and '*little*' which are 0.248, 0.243 and 0.209 respectively whereas lower scores of under 0.2 for '*tiny and very hungry*', '*hungry*', '*stomachache*' and '*feel better*".

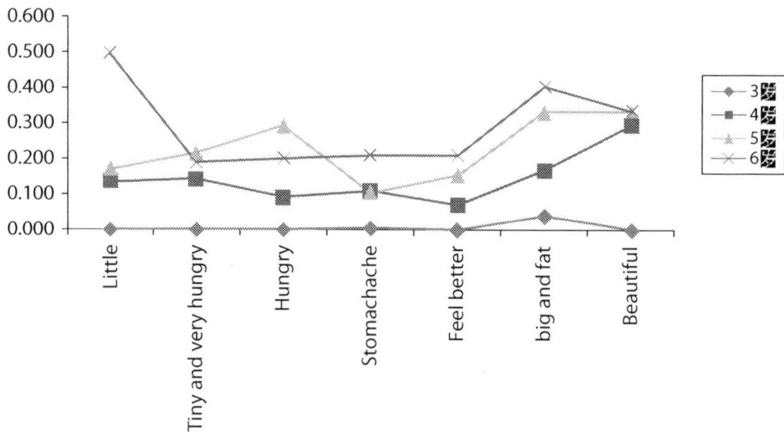

Figure 6. Comparison of score by different SOC

4. Discussion

The three analytical measures integrate 'story grammar' and 'grammar of visual design' and enable us to examine children's comprehension in detail. This is in contrast to published studies such as Paris and Paris (2001, 2003), Lin (1999) and Wagner et al. (1999) who only provide an overview of how many components of story grammar children could use in their retelling after self-reading. The main findings are summarized below.

4.1 General development of children's comprehension of a picture storybook

The results show that the age of 3 to 6 is an important period for children in developing competence in storybook reading comprehension, especially their comprehension of IOP and AE. Paris and Paris (2001, 2003) argue that children aged five to six years could only tell about two out of six items of story grammar in a retelling task, which is much less than older children who have started school. They suggest that children under 6 years old could understand little about a story when reading on their own. However, our study using integrated analytical measures showed that this is not the case. It is found through our data analysis that from the age of three to six, children make significant progress in their comprehension of a storybook. At the age of three, children can understand image of participant to some extent but very little about action event and state of character. However, by six, children's scores on comprehension of IOP, AE and SOC have developed significantly.

4.2 Developing order of children's comprehension of a picture storybook

The data show that children as young as three years old understand some IOP. The comprehension of AE and SOC began to develop around the age of four. In the case of AE, children's comprehension improves very fast from the age of four and nearly catches up with IOP by the age of six. SOC shows a steady increase from 4 to 5 years old, but slows down from 5 years old. These results show that the age of four is a key stage for children's development of comprehension of AE and SOC. In addition, children's reading comprehension of storybooks develops in a certain order: IOP first, AE second and SOC last.

The observed age-related developmental order among the children is consistent with other studies on children's development of language and cognitive ability. First of all, image of participant, as a basic narrative unit of a picture, resembles people and objects in real life explicitly. Therefore, it is easier for young children to recognize (Goldsmith, 1984; Cooper, 2008). Secondly, Action event is represented by relationships between different images of participant which require children to integrate relative information and draw inferences. Children's ability to integrate information and make inference is known to expand rapidly between 4 and 8 years (Paris & Paris, 2001; 2003) and this may partly explain why their comprehension of AE improves from the age of four. Thirdly, to understand state of character, children need to draw inference and empathise with characters, the ability otherwise known as 'theory of mind', which is found to emerge around age 4 to 5 years, and expand only after age 6 years (Wang & Zhang, 2002; Wang, 2000). This may well explain why from 4 years of age children start to understand SOC but comprehension of this develops more slowly than that of IOP and AE.

4.3 Why are some items more difficult for children to comprehend than others?

The data analysis shows that children from different age groups share a good level of consistency in comprehending IOP, AE and SOC in that they tend to comprehend some items more easily than others. To be specific, firstly, images of participant which are either not prominent in a picture or contain culture-specific information with which children are not familiar turned out to be difficult for children to understand (recall that the book was originally published in English). For example, all the children understand '*butterfly*' better than '*caterpillar*' and '*egg*' and '*leaf 2*' better than '*leaf 1*', because '*butterfly*' and '*leaf 2*' are more prominent in the picture. As shown in Figures 7 and 8, which display images in proportion to these images in the storybook; the image of *butterfly* is colourful, sizeable and elaborated, while in contrast, *caterpillar* is colourful yet smaller, and *egg* is very small and painted in white, which could be seen as other possible objects. The dark background of *leaf 1* makes it harder to recognize its outline, whereas leaf 2 is foregrounded by a white background and has a small caterpillar on it.

While the children had little difficulty with images of apple, pear, strawberry and orange, they had great difficulty in understanding the image of plums. This is perhaps due to culture-specific representation. Figure 9 shows the image used for plum in the storybook and photos of plums in the west and China. It is clear that the Victoria plum variety upon which the image in the story book is based is

Figure 7. Images of egg, caterpillar and butterfly

Figure 8. Images of leaf 1 and leaf 2

Figure 9. Images of plum, photos of Victoria plum and Chinese plum

different from a typical plum found in China. The former is purple in colour while the latter is maroon.

Secondly, young children tend to interpret meaning based on explicit information (Goldsmith, 1984) and very often fail to infer implicit meaning in a picture (Cooper, 2008). The children in our study found it difficult to recognize action events which required integrating information from previous and following pictures. Figures 10 and 11 show two examples of AE of different degrees of recognisability: 'ate' and 'look for'. In Figure 10, the AE 'ate' is represented by the relationship between caterpillar and pear (on this page, the caterpillar is going to eat the pear) which has been made explicit in the drawing. In contrast, the AE 'look for' in Figure 11 is not represented explicitly by the picture and children need to infer this meaning from the previous and following pictures. In fact, in the data, many children tried to infer the AE of Figure 11 according to the action of the caterpillar and the relationship between the objects they observed. For example, some children observed, "The caterpillar wants to catch the sun"; "It jumps and wants to catch the sun"; or "The sun falls onto the caterpillar".

Thirdly, in general, young children's ability to understand others' mental state is limited due to their developmental level according to the 'theory of mind' (Wang

Figure 10. AE of "ate" represented explicitly by picture

Figure 11. AE of "look for" represented implicitly by pictures

& Zhang, 2002). Children found it easier to understand characters' states (SOC) represented by visible information such as size and colour than those less visible or age-appropriate. For example, many children were able to retell the states of '*big*', '*fat*' and '*beautiful*', because the *caterpillar* or *butterfly* in the pictures concerned are sizable and colourful enough for children to observe the relative states. Few children, however, understood the states of 'hungry', 'feel better' and 'stomachache', partly because such internal state or feelings are much more difficult to illustrate with an image, and partly because it is also difficult to see the caterpillar's facial expressions and postures in general in the pictures and, in addition, the caterpillar in the 'feel better' picture is much smaller than other items on the same page.

5. Conclusion

To conclude, the study investigates children's comprehension of narrative meaning and meaning-making through pictures in a storybook, using three analytical measures, i.e. images of participants, action event and state of character. It is found that (1) Chinese children's understanding of images, actions and characters' states improves with age; (2) Children develop their understanding of images first, followed by actions and then characters' states; (3) It is easier for children to understand images prominent in pictures than those not prominent in pictures or containing culture-specific information with which children are not familiar, actions represented directly through relationships between different images than those actions which require making connections with preceding and following pictures, and characters' states represented by visible information such as size and colour than those less visible or age-appropriate. There are limitations to this study. For instance, we only analyzed children's reading comprehension of one storybook. Further studies are needed to replicate the investigation on other story books with different styles. Children's development of comprehension of picture books is a continuous and on-going process and subject to linguistic and cognitive factors in addition to their ability to make meaning through pictures. Further studies are needed to explore how these different components of multi-literacy interact with each other in the development of children's reading ability.

References

Bourg, Tammy, Bauer, Patricia & Paul. van den Broek, 1997. "Building the bridges: the development of event comprehension and representation". In *Developmental spans in event comprehension*, eds. Paul van den Broek, Patricia Bauer and Tammy Bourg, 385–407. Mahwah, NJ: Erlbaum.

Carle, Eric. trans. Zheng, J. M. 2008. *The Very Hungry Caterpillar*. Jinan: Tomorrow Publishing House.

Cooper, Linda Z. 2008. "Supporting visual literacy in the school library media Center: Developmental, socio cultural, and experiential considerations and scenarios". *Knowledge Quest / Visual Literacy* 36:3.14–19.

Cope, Bill & Kalantzis, Mary. 2000. *Multiliteracies: Literacy learning and the design of social futures*. London: Routledge

Cope, Bill & Kalantzis, Mary. 2009. "Multiliteracies": New literacies, new learning. *Pedagogies: An international journal* 4.164–195.

Cortazzi, Martin. 2002. *Narrative Analysis*. London: RoutledgeFalmer.

Doonan, Jane. 1993. *Looking at Pictures in Picture Books*. Stroud: Thimble Press.

Edwards, Carolyn Pope & Linda Mayo, Willis. 2000. "Integrating Visual and Verbal Literacies in the early Childhood Classroom". *Early Childhood Education Journal* 27:4.259–265.

Evans, Mary Ann & Jean, Saint-Aubin. 2005. "What children are looking at during shared storybook reading". *Psychological science: a journal of the American Psychological Society* 16:11.913–20.

Gao, Xiao Mei. 2009. *A Study on Eye Movement in the Context of Picture Book Reading for Mandarin-speaking Preschool Children*. Doctorial Dissertation of East China Normal University.

Glenn, Christine G. 1978. "The role of episodic structure of story length in children's recall of simple stories". *Journal of Verbal Learning and Verbal Behaviour* 17.229–47.

Goldsmith, Evelyn. 1984. *Research into illustration: an approach and a review*. New York: Cambridge Univ. Pr.

Jewitt, Carey & Rumiko, Oyama. 2001. "Visual meaning: a social semiotic approach". Leeuwen, Theo Van. & Jewitt, Carey. ed., *Handbook of visual analysis*. 134–156. London: SAGE Publications Ltd.

Justice, Laura M. & Chris, Lankford. 2002. "Preschool children's visual attention to print during storybook reading: Pilot Findings". *Communication Disorders Quarterly* 24:1.11–21.

Justice, Laura, M., Skibbe, Lori, Canning, Andrea & Chris, Lankford. 2005. "Pre-schoolers, print and storybooks: an observational study using eye movement analysis". *Journal of Research in Reading* 28:3.229–243.

Kang, Chang Yun. 2007. *A Study on Picture Storybook Reading Process of Young Children.* Beijing: Educational Science Publishing House.

Kintsch, Walter & Katherine A, Rawson. 2005. "Comprehension". In *The Science of Reading: A Handbook*, ed. Snowling, Margaret J. & Hulme, Charles. 209–226. Oxford: Blackwell Publishing.

Kress, Gunther & Theo Van, Leeuwen. 1996. *Reading Images: The Grammar of Visual Design.* London: Routledge.

Lin, Shu-Min.1999. *The effects of creative drama on story comprehension for children in Taiwan.* Dissertation presented in partial fulfillment of the requirements for the degree doctor of education of Arizona State University.

Lu, Zhong Yi & Dan Lin, Peng. 1990. "An Important Method for Story Comprehension Researching — Story Grammar". *Psychological Science News* 3.44–48.

MacWhinney, Brian. 1991. *The CHILDES project: Computational tools for analyzing talk.* Hillsdale, NJ: Erlbaum.

Mandler, Jean Matter & Nancy S, Johnson. 1977. "Remembrance of things parsed: Story structure and recall". *Cognitive psychology* 9.111–115.

Nicholas, Judy Lavender. 2007. *An Exploration of the Impact of Picture Book Illustrations on the Comprehension Skills and Vocabulary Development of Emergent Readers.* PhD dissertation submitted to Louisiana State University.

Nikolajeva, Maria & Carole, Scott. 2000. "The dynamics of picturebook communication". *Children's Literature in Education* 31:4.225–239.

Nikolajeva, Maria. 2006. "Verbal and visual literacy: the role of picturebooks in the reading experience of young children", in *Handbook of Early Childhood Literacy*, ed. Hall, Nigel. Larson, Joanne & Marsh, Jackie. 235–248. London: SAGE Publications.

Nodelman, Perry. 1988. *Words about Pictures: the Narrative Art of Children's Picture Books.* Athens, GA: University of Georgia Press.

Paris, Alison H. & Scott G, Paris. 2001. *Children's Comprehension of Narrative Picture Books.* CIERA Report.

Paris, Alison H. & Scott G. Paris. 2003."Assessing narrative comprehension in young children". *Reading Research Quarterly* 38:1.36–76.

Roy-Charland, Annie, Saint-Aubin, Jean & Mary Ann, Evans. 2007. "Eye movements in shared book reading with children from kindergarten to Grade 4". *Reading and Writing* 20:9.909–931.

Rumelhart, David Everett. 1975. "Notes on a schema for stories" in *Representation and Understanding: Studies in Cognitive Science*, ed. Bobrow, Daniel Gureasko & Collins, Allan. 211–236. London: Academic Press.

Rumelhart, David Everett. 1977. "Understanding and summarizing brief stories". In *Basic Processes in Reading: perception and Comprehension*, ed. Laberge, Davide & Samuels, S. Jay, 263–303.New York: Wiley.

Schwarcz, Joseph H. 1982. "Ways of the Illustrator: Visual Communication". In *Children's Literature.* Chicago: American Library Association.

Stein, Nancy L. & Christine G, Glenn. 1979. "An analysis of story comprehension in elementary school children". In *New Directions in Discourse Processing*, ed. Freedle, Roy O. Norwood, NJ: Ablex.

Stewig, John W. 1995. *Looking at Picture Books*. Fort Atkinson, WI: Highsmith.

Thorndyke, Perry W. 1977. "Cognitive structures in comprehension and memory of narrative discourse", *Cognitive Psychology* 9:1.77–110.

Unsworth, Len & Janet, Wheeler. 2002. "Re-valuing the role of images in reviewing picture books". *Literacy (formerly Reading)* 36:2.68–74.

Wagner, C.R. Sahln, B. & U, Nettelbladt.1999. "Narration and comprehension in Swedish pre-school children". *Child language teaching and therapy* 15.13–137.

Wang, Yi Wen & Wen Xin, Zhang. 2002. "Development of "Theory of Mind" of Children from 3 to 6 Years Old". *Development and Education of Psychology* 1.11–15

Wang, Zhen Yu. 2000.*Theory of Children's Psychology Development*. Shanghai: East China Normal University Press.

Williams, T. Lee. 2007. "'Reading' the painting: Exploring visual literacy in the primary grades". *The Reading Teacher* 60:7.636–642.

Woolley, Gary. 2010. "Developing reading comprehension: Combining visual and verbal cognitive processes". *Australian Journal of Language and Literacy* 33:2.108–125.

About the authors

GAO Xiaomei is Director of Zizhu Kindergarten attached to East China Normal University. Her main research interests are monolingual and bilingual children's language development and education, and early literacy development and education.

Chiung-chih HUANG is Professor of Linguistics at National Chengchi University, Taiwan. Her research interests include the development of conversational skills and the relationship between discourse pragmatics and grammar in child language. Her recent studies include longitudinal investigations of Mandarin-speaking children's referential choice in natural conversation from a discourse-pragmatic perspective.

Lixian JIN is Chair Professor of Linguistics and Intercultural Learning at De Montfort University, UK. Her research and publications are in cultures of learning, ELT, intercultural communication, clinical linguistic assessments, metaphor and narrative analysis. She is an editor on international journals, including International Journal of Language and Communication Disorders.

Zhuo JING-SCHMIDT is Associate Professor of Chinese linguistics at the University of Oregon. She teaches and researches language structure, use, and change, and cognition and emotion in language, as well as second language acquisition. With scholarly experiences in three continents, she publishes in English, German, and Chinese.

Shing On LEUNG is Associate Professor of education in Faculty of Education, University of Macau. His teaching and research areas are in educational measurement and applications of statistics in education social sciences. He also served various key educational research projects in Hong Kong including the Academic Aptitude Test in 1996.

Hui LI is an Associate Professor of Early Childhood Language and Education in the Faculty of Education at The University of Hong Kong. His teaching and research interests are in Early Language and Literacy and Early Childhood Education. He has published altogether 138 articles, books, chapters, commentaries, and monographs.

LI Linhui is Lecturer in Preschool Education at the College of Education of Shanghai Normal University. Her main research interests are preschool children's language development and education, early literacy development and education, and preschool children's communication during play.

LIU Baogen is Lecturer in Preschool Education at Hangzhou Kindergarten Teacher College of Zhejiang Normal University. His main research interests are preschool children's language development and education, and early literacy development and education.

Shek Kam TSE is Director of Centre for the Advancement of Chinese Language Education and Research, HKU; an educational consultant, including to the Netherlands, Singapore and Hong Kong. His research interests include Chinese Language teaching and learning, early childhood language and language assessment with 100 research articles and 55 books.

Jing ZHOU is Professor, Director of ESEC Child Language Research Center (CLRC) at East China Normal University and Head of CLRC of China National Society of Early Childhood Education. She has been conducting cross-national studies in Chinese children's language development and education with 20 books and many academic papers.

ZHU Hua is Chair Professor in Applied Linguistics and Communication at Birkbeck College, University of London. Her main research interests are phonological development by monolingual and bilingual children, intercultural pragmatics, and language and intercultural communication. Her most recent book-length publication is Exploring Intercultural Communication: Language in Action (published by Routledge).

Index